MANOR ELEMENTARY SCHOOL
PENN VALLEY ROAD
LEVITTOWN, PENNSYLVANIA

000068

macmillan
mathematics

Tina Thoburn, Senior Author

Jack E. Forbes, Senior Author

Robert D. Bechtel

Macmillan Publishing Company
New York

Collier Macmillan Publishers
London

GRAPHIC CONCERN, INC.

Designer: Stanley Konopka

Cover Photography: Arthur Beck

Production Project Manager: Ruth Riley

Technical Art: Dave Hannum, Phil Jones

Illustrations: Olivia Cole 2-3, 10-11, 22, 72, 81, 83, 98 bottom, 133, 134, 266, 356, 418, 420 / Len Ebert 27, 30, 31, 58, 60-61, 66-67, 74-75, 90, 91, 106, 107, 123, 146, 154, 169, 180, 181, 199, 208 top, 213, 228, 229, 239, 240, 249, 270, 291, 318 / Angela Fernan 11, 103, 120, 143, 171, 243, 302, 329, 349 / Tony Fiyalko 96, 101, 113, 132, 157, 251, 298 / Fuka 13, 14, 23, 68, 114, 120, 136, 137, 166, 167, 198, 203, 212, 244, 247, 268, 312, 357 / Donald Gates 149 / Susan Gray 34 / Will Harmuth 2-3, 41, 62 / Michael O'Reilly 115 / Jan Palmer 18-19, 98 top, 104 / Tom Powers 29, 34, 94, 95, 141, 163, 173, 174, 175, 233, 264, 265, 303, 304, 372 / Jan Pyk 122, 148, 158, 176, 234, 296 / Nancy Schill 85, 114, 132, 316, 361 / Joel Snyder 36-37, 54, 55, 109, 117, 121, 139 / Lynn Uhde 45, 52, 53, 144, 145, 156, 159, 178-179, 187, 196-197, 202, 254, 280, 283, 301 / Gary Undercuffler 108, 182, 236, 300, 374 / Sally Jo Vitsky 78-79, 262, 263 / John Wallner 41, 89, 99, 155, 182 / Lane Yerkes 9, 65, 85, 88, 150, 170, 216, 288-289, 309.

Photography: Clara Aich Photography, 80, 252, 253, 388, 415; Apple Computer Inc. 378; E.S. Bernard/ Shostal Assoc. 295; The Bettman Archive, Inc. 373, 377; Jay Brenner 130, 208 bottom; P. Costas/ Shostal Assoc. 245, 275; D'Arazien/Shostal Assoc. 9, 143; E.R. Degginger 25; J. Dimaggio, J. Kalish/ Image Bank 195; R. Forbes/The Image Bank 273; Lawrence Fried/The Image Bank, 379; I. Gruttner 6, 7, 33, 48, 50, 92, 101, 143, 147, 206, 210, 216, 217, 272, 273, 275, 276, 277, 279, 293, 349; W. Hamilton/Shostal Assoc. 1; K. Hayes 14, 16, 111, 253; D. Herman/Shostal Assoc. 269; M. Heron 59, 153, 271; T. Hopker/Woodfin Camp 165; Image Bank 47, 311: R. Morsch 10, 17, 26, 71, 93, 100, 110, 116, 118, 119, 129, 130, 131, 132, 133, 134, 135, 152, 153, 160, 162, 177, 188, 204, 209, 255, 267, 287, 299, 318; M.E. Newman/ Woodfin Camp 87, 200; Alvis Upitis/Shostal Assoc. 341; J. Zehrt/Shostal Assoc. 261.

Parts of this work were published in earlier editions of SERIES M: Macmillan Mathematics.

Macmillan Publishing Company
866 Third Avenue
New York, N.Y. 10022
Collier Macmillan Canada, Inc.

Printed in the United States of America

ISBN 0-02-103490-7
9 8 7 6 5 4 3

contents

MULTIPLICATION AND DIVISION   **UNIT 4**

MONEY, TIME, MEASUREMENT   **UNIT 5**

MULTIPLYING BY ONES   **UNIT 6**

MID-YEAR REVIEW   **189-194**

GEOMETRY

DECIMALS

END-YEAR REVIEW

COMPUTER LITERACY

SPECIAL TOPICS

WORKBOOK

Reviewing Addition and Subtraction Facts

1

Addition Facts

A. The Comet has 8 cars.
In Chicago, 7 more cars are attached.
How many cars are now on the Comet?

You can **add** to find how many in all.

$$\begin{array}{r} 8 \\ +7 \\ \hline 15 \end{array} \qquad 8 + 7 = 15$$

There are now 15 cars.

B. The numbers you add are called the **addends.**
The answer is called the **sum.**

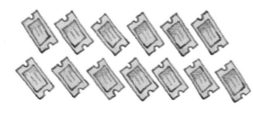

$$\begin{array}{r} 6 \\ +7 \\ \hline 13 \end{array} \text{addends} \qquad \underset{\text{addends}}{6 + 7} = \underset{\text{sum}}{13}$$

13 ← sum

TRY THESE

Add to find the sums.

1. $\begin{array}{r} 8 \\ +5 \\ \hline 13 \end{array}$

2. $\begin{array}{r} 7 \\ +9 \\ \hline 16 \end{array}$

3. $\begin{array}{r} 9 \\ +6 \\ \hline 15 \end{array}$

4. $\begin{array}{r} 4 \\ +5 \\ \hline 9 \end{array}$

5. $\begin{array}{r} 7 \\ +6 \\ \hline 13 \end{array}$

6. $\begin{array}{r} 4 \\ +7 \\ \hline 11 \end{array}$

7. $\begin{array}{r} 6 \\ +8 \\ \hline 14 \end{array}$

8. $\begin{array}{r} 9 \\ +7 \\ \hline 16 \end{array}$

9. $\begin{array}{r} 9 \\ +9 \\ \hline 18 \end{array}$

SKILLS PRACTICE

Add.

1.   3
   +8
   ―――
   11

2.   8
   +7
   ―――
   15

3.   7
   +7
   ―――
   14

4.   5
   +6
   ―――
   11

5.   7
   +3
   ―――
   10

6.   4
   +9
   ―――
   13

7.   8
   +6
   ―――
   14

8.   5
   +8
   ―――
   13

9.   6
   +4
   ―――
   10

10.   9
    +6
   ―――
    15

11.   8
    +5
   ―――
    13

12.   8
    +4
   ―――
    12

13.   2
    +6
   ―――
    8

14.   2
    +8
   ―――
    10

15.   6
    +7
   ―――
    13

16.   7
    +9
   ―――
    16

17.   6
    +5
   ―――
    11

18.   8
    +3
   ―――
    11

19.   3
    +6
   ―――
    9

20.   5
    +9
   ―――
    14

21.   7
    +8
   ―――
    15

22.   9
    +2
   ―――
    11

23.   9
    +7
   ―――
    16

24.   7
    +5
   ―――
    12

25.   6
    +6
   ―――
    12

26.   4
    +8
   ―――
    12

27.   0
    +9
   ―――
    9

28.   9
    +3
   ―――
    12

29.   1
    +8
   ―――
    9

30.   9
    +9
   ―――
    18

31. 6 + 8 = ▪ 14

32. 2 + 9 = ▪ 11

33. 0 + 8 = ▪ 8

34. 5 + 7 = ▪ 12

35. 8 + 9 = ▪ 17

36. 9 + 5 = ▪ 14

37. Add 5 and 9. 14

38. Find the sum of 7 and 8. 15

★ 39. One addend is 4. The sum is 11. What is the other addend? 7

PROBLEM SOLVING

The train conductor kept a record of people who bought their tickets on the train on four days. Copy the record and find the totals.

	Between NYC and Rye	Between Rye and Stamford	Total
40.	8	1	9
41.	6	4	10
42.	6	7	13
43.	3	9	12

Addition Properties

Special properties of addition can help you find sums.

$$\begin{array}{r} 9 \\ +6 \\ \hline 15 \end{array} \qquad \begin{array}{r} 6 \\ +9 \\ \hline 15 \end{array}$$

When you change the order of the addends, the sum does not change.

Order Property

$$\begin{array}{r} 0 \\ +9 \\ \hline 9 \end{array} \qquad \begin{array}{r} 3 \\ +0 \\ \hline 3 \end{array}$$

When one addend is 0, the sum is the other addend.

Zero Property

$$\begin{array}{r} 3 \\ 2 \\ +4 \\ \hline 9 \end{array} \quad \begin{array}{c} 5 \\ \\ +4 \\ \hline 9 \end{array} \qquad \begin{array}{r} 3 \\ 2 \\ +4 \\ \hline 9 \end{array} \quad \begin{array}{c} 3 \\ \\ +6 \\ \hline 9 \end{array}$$

When you group addends in a different way, the sum is the same.

Grouping Property

$$9 + 4 = 13$$

When a fact is written in this form, it is called a **number sentence.**

TRY THESE

Find the sums.

1. $\begin{array}{r} 2 \\ +9 \\ \hline 11 \end{array}$ **2.** $\begin{array}{r} 9 \\ +2 \\ \hline 11 \end{array}$ **3.** $\begin{array}{r} 4 \\ +8 \\ \hline 12 \end{array}$ **4.** $\begin{array}{r} 8 \\ +4 \\ \hline 12 \end{array}$ **5.** $\begin{array}{r} 8 \\ +7 \\ \hline 15 \end{array}$ **6.** $\begin{array}{r} 7 \\ +8 \\ \hline 15 \end{array}$

7. $\begin{array}{r} 6 \\ +0 \\ \hline 6 \end{array}$ **8.** $\begin{array}{r} 0 \\ +3 \\ \hline 3 \end{array}$ **9.** $\begin{array}{r} 0 \\ +0 \\ \hline 0 \end{array}$ **10.** $\begin{array}{r} 6 \\ 2 \\ +3 \\ \hline 11 \end{array}$ **11.** $\begin{array}{r} 4 \\ 4 \\ +4 \\ \hline 12 \end{array}$ **12.** $\begin{array}{r} 5 \\ 4 \\ +1 \\ \hline 10 \end{array}$ **13.** $\begin{array}{r} 2 \\ 6 \\ +2 \\ \hline 10 \end{array}$

Complete the number sentences.

14. $9 + 7 = $ ■ 16   **15.** $7 + 6 = $ ■ 13   **16.** $6 + 4 = $ ■ 10

SKILLS PRACTICE

Add.

1. 8
   +5
   13

2. 6
   +6
   12

3. 4
   +5
   9

4. 5
   +4
   9

5. 9
   +9
   18

6. 5
   +5
   10

7. 9
   +0
   9

8. 5
   +9
   14

9. 9
   +5
   14

10. 0
   +7
   7

11. 9
   +8
   17

12. 1
   +9
   10

13. 7
   +7
   14

14. 9
   +4
   13

15. 8
   +8
   16

16. 2
   +8
   10

17. 9
   +6
   15

18. 3
   +8
   11

19. 8
   +3
   11

20. 3
   +9
   12

21. 6
   +7
   13

22. 7
   +9
   16

23. 6
   +8
   14

24. 8
   +6
   14

25. 8
   +9
   17

26. 8
   +0
   8

27. 0
   +9
   9

28. 4
   +6
   10

29. 1
    6
    +2
    9

30. 3
    3
    +3
    9

31. 5
    0
    +4
    9

32. 4
    1
    +4
    9

33. 5
    2
    +3
    10

34. 3
    4
    +5
    12

35. 4
    2
    +2
    8

Complete the number sentences.

36. $5 + 7 = $ ■ 12

37. $0 + 6 = $ ■ 6

38. $7 + 4 = $ ■ 11

39. $3 + 2 + 6 = $ ■ 11

40. $4 + 4 + 2 = $ ■ 10

41. $5 + 3 + 1 = $ ■ 9

42. $1 + 8 + 1 = $ ■ 10

★43. $276 + 0 = $ ■ 276

★44. $0 + 489 = $ ■ 489

EXTRA! Making Logical Choices

The 10 pens in a box look exactly alike. However, 4 have red ink
and 6 have blue ink. How many pens would you have to select
to be *sure* that you have:

At least 2 with ink of the same color?

At least 2 with red ink?

At least 2 with blue ink?

Problem Solving: A 5-Step Plan

These five steps can help you solve problems.

1 Read the problem.

The librarian put 9 books in the bookcase.
Then he put 2 more books in the bookcase.
How many books were in the bookcase?

2 Plan what to do.

I need to find how many in all.

9 books there. 2 more put with them. Add to find how many in all.

$$9 + 2 = \blacksquare$$

3 Do the arithmetic.

$$\begin{array}{r} 9 \\ +2 \\ \hline 11 \end{array}$$

4 Give the answer.

There were 11 books in the bookcase.

5 Check your answer.

Use the Order Property.

$$\begin{array}{r} 2 \\ +9 \\ \hline 11 \checkmark \end{array}$$

TRY THESE

Could you *add* to solve these problems? Answer *yes* or *no*.

1. Ed had 9 music magazines. Ines had 2. How many did they have all together? yes

2. Maria took 9 books from the library. She gave 2 books to her sister. How many books did she have left? No

3. There were 9 people in the library. 2 of the people went home. How many people were left in the library? No

4. Jim read 9 books last month and 2 books this month. How many books did he read in all? Yes

PROBLEM SOLVING PRACTICE

Use the five steps to solve each problem.

1. There were 7 people in the library. Then 2 more people came into the library. How many people were in the library then? 9

2. Kathy signed out 2 books to do her science report and 2 books to do her English report. How many books did she sign out? 4

3. José used 7 pages for his science report. Charles used only 4 pages. How many pages did they use all together? 11

4. Sarah read 8 pages of a mystery story before lunch and 9 pages after lunch. How many pages did she read in all? 17

5. The library bought one book about wild flowers for $9 and another book about wild flowers for $7. How much did the library pay for these books? 16

6. The librarian used 3 meters of string to tie up one box of books. He used 5 meters of string to tie up another box. How many meters of string did he use? 8

7. Six names were on the waiting list for a book. Four people added their names to the list. How many names were on the list then? 10

8. Sam took out 3 horse books, 2 sports books, and 1 joke book. How many books did Sam take out? 6

★9. Nine people took out books before 3 o'clock and 8 other people took out books after 3 o'clock. How many people in all took out books? 17

★10. Juanita returned 5 books on October 3 and 6 books on October 9. How many books did Juanita return? 11

Make up a word problem for each number sentence.

★11. 7 + 6 = 13

There were 7 cookies in the the the jar. Nancy put 6 cookies in the jar. How many cookies were in the jar? 13

★12. 4 + 2 + 3 = 9

Nancy read 4 pages in her book. The next day she read 2 pages, and next day she read three pages. How many pages did she read?

Add.

1. 5 +4 9	**2.** 7 +0 7	**3.** 9 +2 11	**4.** 7 +3 10	**5.** 3 +9 12	**6.** 2 +7 9	**7.** 9 +6 15
8. 2 +0 2	**9.** 6 +8 14	**10.** 5 +6 11	**11.** 6 +9 15	**12.** 8 +7 15	**13.** 9 +8 17	**14.** 1 +3 4
15. 9 +9 18	**16.** 8 +6 14	**17.** 4 +3 7	**18.** 9 +4 13	**19.** 5 +8 13	**20.** 5 +1 6	**21.** 8 +5 13
22. 6 +3 9	**23.** 7 +7 14	**24.** 7 +4 11	**25.** 2 +9 11	**26.** 4 +8 12	**27.** 9 +7 16	**28.** 8 +4 12
29. 4 +9 13	**30.** 6 +5 11	**31.** 7 +6 13	**32.** 8 +8 16	**33.** 0 +4 4	**34.** 8 +9 17	**35.** 9 +3 12
36. 5 4 +4 13	**37.** 1 2 +7 10	**38.** 6 3 +2 11	**39.** 4 3 +1 8	**40.** 8 1 +1 10	**41.** 3 5 +1 9	**42.** 7 1 +0 8

Complete the number sentences.

43. 7 + 1 = 8

44. 3 + 8 = 11

45. 5 + 9 = 14

46. 8 + 3 = 11

47. 6 + 7 = 13

48. 7 + 8 = 15

49. 9 + 5 = 14

50. 7 + 9 = 16

51. 3 + 2 = 5

52. 5 + 1 + 3 = 9

53. 2 + 2 + 2 = 6

54. 4 + 3 + 2 = 9

Solve the problems.

55. There were 5 basketball players on one team and 5 basketball players on the other team. How many players were there in all? 10

56. There were 9 baseball players on one team and 9 baseball players on the other team. How many players were there in all? 18

Project: Completing a Table

An inspector at a toy factory graded each toy robot on how it looked and how it worked.

The highest grade for how it looks is 9.
The lowest grade for how it looks is 0.

The highest grade for how it works is 9.
The lowest grade for how it works is 0.

The inspector added the two grades together to get a total score for each robot. You can use this table to show all possible scores.

$$\begin{array}{r} 3 \\ +5 \\ \hline 8 \end{array}$$

$$\begin{array}{r} 7 \\ +8 \\ \hline 15 \end{array}$$

WORKS

+	0	1	2	3	4	5	6	7	8	9
0	0	1	2	3	4	5	6	7	8	9
1	1	2	3	4	5	6	7	8	9	10
2	2	3	4	5	6	7	8	9	10	11
3	3	4	5	6	7	8	9	10	11	12
4	4	5	6	7	8	9	10	11	12	13
5	5	6	7	8	9	10	11	12	13	14
6	6	7	8	9	10	11	12	13	14	15
7	7	8	9	10	11	12	13	14	15	16
8	8	9	10	11	12	13	14	15	16	17
9	9	10	11	12	13	14	15	16	17	18

(Left side of table labeled **LOOKS**)

1. Copy and complete the table.
2. Look at your completed table.
   0 appears 1 time.
   1 appears 2 times.
   2 appears 3 times.
   3 appears 4 times.
Find how often each sum 4–18 appears.

Grade some fruits or vegetables on how they taste. Use 0–9. Then grade them on how they look. Give each a total score.

Subtraction Facts

A. Andy had 12 black checkers.
Karen won 4 of them.
How many black checkers
does Andy have left? 8

You can **subtract** to find
how many are left.

$$12 \qquad 12 - 4 = 8$$
$$\underline{-\ 4}$$
$$8$$

Andy has 8 black checkers left.

B. The answer to a subtraction is called the **difference.**

$$11 \qquad\qquad 11 - 6 = 5$$
$$\underline{-\ 6} \qquad\qquad\qquad \uparrow$$
$$5 \leftarrow \text{difference} \qquad\qquad \textbf{difference}$$

TRY THESE _____

Subtract to find the differences.

1. $\begin{array}{r} 13 \\ -\ 4 \\ \hline 9 \end{array}$

2. $\begin{array}{r} 15 \\ -\ 7 \\ \hline 8 \end{array}$

3. $\begin{array}{r} 13 \\ -\ 5 \\ \hline 8 \end{array}$
4. $\begin{array}{r} 11 \\ -\ 8 \\ \hline 3 \end{array}$
5. $\begin{array}{r} 14 \\ -\ 9 \\ \hline 5 \end{array}$
6. $\begin{array}{r} 11 \\ -\ 4 \\ \hline 7 \end{array}$
7. $\begin{array}{r} 13 \\ -\ 7 \\ \hline 6 \end{array}$
8. $\begin{array}{r} 9 \\ -0 \\ \hline 9 \end{array}$
9. $\begin{array}{r} 16 \\ -\ 9 \\ \hline 7 \end{array}$

10   **Reviewing Addition and Subtraction Facts**

SKILLS PRACTICE

Subtract.

1. 16 − 9 = 7

2. 18 − 9 = 9

3. 12 − 6 = 6
4. 15 − 7 = 8
5. 14 − 7 = 7
6. 11 − 2 = 8
7. 10 − 3 = 7
8. 15 − 9 = 6
9. 11 − 9 = 2

10. 13 − 6 = 7
11. 12 − 8 = 4
12. 11 − 3 = 8
13. 9 − 8 = 1
14. 15 − 6 = 9
15. 12 − 5 = 7
16. 13 − 7 = 6

17. 10 − 6 = 4
18. 12 − 7 = 5
19. 11 − 7 = 4
20. 0 − 0 = 0
21. 14 − 8 = 6
22. 11 − 4 = 7
23. 10 − 8 = 2

24. 14 − 9 = 5
25. 11 − 5 = 6
26. 12 − 9 = 3
27. 13 − 5 = 8
28. 12 − 3 = 9
29. 16 − 8 = 8
30. 13 − 4 = 9

31. 10 − 9 = ▦ 1

32. 14 − 6 = ▦ 8

33. 9 − 4 = ▦ 5

34. 17 − 8 = ▦ 9

35. 11 − 8 = ▦ 3

36. 13 − 8 = ▦ 5

37. Subtract 7 from 12. 3

38. Find the difference of 17 and 8. 9

★ 39. Subtract a number from itself. What is the difference? 0

PROBLEM SOLVING

Follow the instructions to reach HOME FREE.

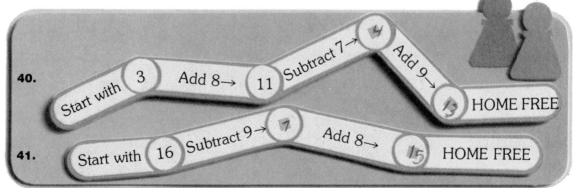

40. Start with 3 — Add 8→ 11 — Subtract 7→ 4 — Add 9→ 13 — HOME FREE

41. Start with 16 — Subtract 9→ 7 — Add 8→ 15 — HOME FREE

Subtraction Properties

Special properties of subtraction can help you find differences.

$$\begin{array}{r} 3 \\ -3 \\ \hline 0 \end{array} \qquad \begin{array}{r} 8 \\ -8 \\ \hline 0 \end{array}$$ When you subtract a number from itself, the difference is 0.

Zero in Subtraction

$$\begin{array}{r} 2 \\ -0 \\ \hline 2 \end{array} \qquad \begin{array}{r} 5 \\ -0 \\ \hline 5 \end{array}$$ When you subtract 0 from a number, the difference is that same number.

$$\begin{array}{r} 14 \\ -\ 6 \\ \hline 8 \end{array} \qquad \begin{array}{r} 8 \\ +6 \\ \hline 14 \end{array}$$ Addition and subtraction are related. You can use an addition to check a subtraction.

Checking Subtraction

$15 - 7 = 8$ When a fact is written in this form, it is called a *number sentence.*

TRY THESE

Find the differences.

1. $\begin{array}{r}2\\-2\\\hline 0\end{array}$	**2.** $\begin{array}{r}4\\-4\\\hline 0\end{array}$	**3.** $\begin{array}{r}7\\-7\\\hline 0\end{array}$	**4.** $\begin{array}{r}0\\-0\\\hline 0\end{array}$	**5.** $\begin{array}{r}1\\-0\\\hline 1\end{array}$	**6.** $\begin{array}{r}5\\-0\\\hline 5\end{array}$	**7.** $\begin{array}{r}9\\-0\\\hline 9\end{array}$

Subtract. Then use addition to check your subtraction.

8. $\begin{array}{r}10\\-\ 4\\\hline 6\end{array}$	**9.** $\begin{array}{r}12\\-\ 5\\\hline 7\end{array}$	**10.** $\begin{array}{r}8\\-0\\\hline 8\end{array}$	**11.** $\begin{array}{r}6\\-6\\\hline 0\end{array}$	**12.** $\begin{array}{r}10\\-\ 1\\\hline 9\end{array}$	**13.** $\begin{array}{r}11\\-\ 6\\\hline 5\end{array}$	**14.** $\begin{array}{r}17\\-\ 8\\\hline 9\end{array}$

Complete the number sentences.

15. $10 - 2 = $ 8   **16.** $16 - 7 = $ 9   **17.** $15 - 8 = $ 7

SKILLS PRACTICE _____

Subtract. Use addition to check your subtraction.

1. $\begin{array}{r} 9 \\ -0 \\ \hline 9 \end{array}$
2. $\begin{array}{r} 16 \\ -8 \\ \hline 8 \end{array}$
3. $\begin{array}{r} 12 \\ -9 \\ \hline 3 \end{array}$
4. $\begin{array}{r} 13 \\ -7 \\ \hline 6 \end{array}$
5. $\begin{array}{r} 12 \\ -4 \\ \hline 8 \end{array}$
6. $\begin{array}{r} 13 \\ -9 \\ \hline 4 \end{array}$
7. $\begin{array}{r} 12 \\ -6 \\ \hline 6 \end{array}$

8. $\begin{array}{r} 14 \\ -7 \\ \hline 7 \end{array}$
9. $\begin{array}{r} 15 \\ -8 \\ \hline 7 \end{array}$
10. $\begin{array}{r} 6 \\ -0 \\ \hline 6 \end{array}$
11. $\begin{array}{r} 11 \\ -2 \\ \hline 9 \end{array}$
12. $\begin{array}{r} 9 \\ -9 \\ \hline 0 \end{array}$
13. $\begin{array}{r} 16 \\ -9 \\ \hline 7 \end{array}$
14. $\begin{array}{r} 11 \\ -5 \\ \hline 6 \end{array}$

15. $\begin{array}{r} 13 \\ -6 \\ \hline 7 \end{array}$
16. $\begin{array}{r} 8 \\ -8 \\ \hline 0 \end{array}$
17. $\begin{array}{r} 12 \\ -8 \\ \hline 4 \end{array}$
18. $\begin{array}{r} 11 \\ -3 \\ \hline 8 \end{array}$
19. $\begin{array}{r} 13 \\ -8 \\ \hline 5 \end{array}$
20. $\begin{array}{r} 14 \\ -8 \\ \hline 6 \end{array}$
21. $\begin{array}{r} 12 \\ -3 \\ \hline 9 \end{array}$

Complete the number sentences.

22. $11 - 4 = \blacksquare\,7$
23. $9 - 0 = \blacksquare\,9$
24. $6 - 6 = \blacksquare\,0$

25. $12 - 5 = \blacksquare\,7$
26. $11 - 9 = \blacksquare\,3$
27. $16 - 7 = \blacksquare\,9$

28. $14 - 9 = \blacksquare\,5$
★29. $48 - 48 = \blacksquare\,0$
★30. $64 - 0 = \blacksquare\,64$

Add or subtract.

31. $\begin{array}{r} 9 \\ +8 \\ \hline 17 \end{array}$
32. $\begin{array}{r} 7 \\ -3 \\ \hline 4 \end{array}$
33. $\begin{array}{r} 14 \\ -5 \\ \hline 9 \end{array}$
34. $\begin{array}{r} 11 \\ -7 \\ \hline 4 \end{array}$
35. $\begin{array}{r} 4 \\ +9 \\ \hline 13 \end{array}$
36. $\begin{array}{r} 12 \\ -7 \\ \hline 5 \end{array}$
37. $\begin{array}{r} 17 \\ -9 \\ \hline 8 \end{array}$

38. $\begin{array}{r} 15 \\ -9 \\ \hline 6 \end{array}$
39. $\begin{array}{r} 7 \\ +4 \\ \hline 11 \end{array}$
40. $\begin{array}{r} 13 \\ -5 \\ \hline 8 \end{array}$
41. $\begin{array}{r} 6 \\ +6 \\ \hline 12 \end{array}$
42. $\begin{array}{r} 18 \\ -9 \\ \hline 9 \end{array}$
43. $\begin{array}{r} 8 \\ +7 \\ \hline 15 \end{array}$
44. $\begin{array}{r} 11 \\ -8 \\ \hline 3 \end{array}$

EXTRA!   Using a Calculator

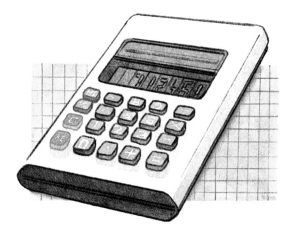

Tell which button or buttons you would push on the calculator for each ●.

Example: $9 \blacktriangleleft 6 = 3$ Answer: −

$11 \blacktriangleleft 4 = 7$ $13 \blacktriangleleft 5 = 8$

$9 \blacktriangleleft 8 = 17$ $6 + 3 \blacktriangleleft 5 = 4$

$7 + 2 \blacktriangleleft 9$ $\bullet\ \blacktriangleleft - 8 = 9$

Problem Solving: Uses of Subtraction

Remember the five steps for solving problems.

1 Read the problem.
2 Plan what to do.
3 Do the arithmetic.
4 Give the answer.
5 Check your answer.

Subtraction gives the answer to many different questions.

A. You can subtract to find *how many are left.*

Jean put 10 jacks on the floor.
She picked up 6 jacks.

How many jacks are left on the floor?

$10 - 6 = $ ▮

$$\begin{array}{r} 10 \\ -\ 6 \\ \hline 4 \end{array}$$

B. You can subtract to find *how many more are needed.*

Mike needs 10 jacks to play.
He has 6 jacks.

How many more jacks does he need?

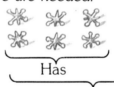

Has

Needs in all

$10 - 6 = $ ▮

$$\begin{array}{r} 10 \\ -\ 6 \\ \hline 4 \end{array}$$

C. You can subtract to find *how many more are in one set than in another.*

Jean has 10 jacks.
Mike has 6 jacks.

How many more jacks does Jean have?

$10 - 6 = $ ▮

$$\begin{array}{r} 10 \\ -\ 6 \\ \hline 4 \end{array}$$

D. Subtraction also answers these questions.

Jean put 10 jacks on the floor. She took away some jacks. 6 jacks are left. *How many jacks did she take away?* 4

Jean has 10 jacks. 6 of the jacks are silver. The other jacks are not silver. *How many jacks are not silver?* 4

Jean has 10 jacks. Mike has 6 jacks. *How many fewer jacks does Mike have?* 4

What must you find?

A. How many are left?
B. How many more are needed?
C. How many more are in one set than in another?

1. Jeff had 16 marbles. He lost 9 marbles. How many marbles does he have left? 7

2. Jeff had 16 marbles. Judy had 9 marbles. How many more marbles did Jeff have? 7

3. Jeff needs 16 marbles to win the game. He has 9 marbles. How many more marbles does he need? 7

4. Jeff had 16 marbles in a bag. He took out 9 marbles. How many marbles were in the bag then? 7

PROBLEM SOLVING PRACTICE _____

Use the five steps to solve each problem.

1. Gail had 12 checkers. She lost 4 checkers. How many checkers did she have left? 8

2. Doug had 9 checkers. Patty had 3 checkers. How many more checkers did Doug have? 6

3. To win the game, Dominic needed to take twelve checkers. He already has taken eight checkers. How many more does he need? 4

4. Ron had 16 checkers. 7 of the checkers were red. The rest of the checkers were black. How many black checkers did he have? 9

5. Rita won 17 games. Ron won 8 games. How many fewer games did Ron win? 9

6. Jim had 12 checkers, but he lost some. He has only 9 checkers left. How many checkers did he lose? 3

★7. There are 14 students in the room. Eight students are playing checkers. The others are playing chess. How many students are playing chess? 6 Are more students playing chess or checkers? chess

★8. Linda won 18 games. Kathy won 9 games. Joan won 15 games. Who won the most games? How many more games than Kathy did she win? Linda 9

Make up a word problem for each number sentence.

★9. $13 - 8 = $ ▪

★10. $16 - 9 = $ ▪

Problem Solving: Choosing the Operation

You can draw a picture to help you choose the operation.

A. While on vacation, Tom sent 4 postcards. Lynn sent 3 postcards. How many postcards did they send? 7

Tom:

Lynn: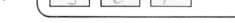

SENT

Add to find how many in all.

```
   4
 + 3
 ___
   7
```
They sent 7 postcards.

B. Carmen bought 7 cards and sent some of them to her friends. She has 5 cards left. How many cards did she send? 2

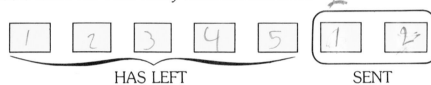

HAS LEFT   SENT

Subtract to find how many she sent.

```
   7
 - 5
 ___
   2
```
Carmen sent 2 cards.

C. Ron sent 4 cards. Rosa sent 7 cards. How many fewer cards did Ron send? 3

Rosa: 7

↕   ↕   ↕   ↕

Ron:

Subtract to find how many fewer Ron sent.

```
   7
 - 4
 ___
   3
```
Ron sent 3 fewer cards.

TRY THESE

Would you *add* or *subtract*? Draw a picture if needed.

1. Jim bought some postcards. He sent some of them to his friends. How many does he have left? 4

2. Luis has collected some pictures. Nancy has collected some pictures, too. How many more pictures does Luis have? 3

3. Ann visited some states last summer and some more states this summer. How many states did she visit? 50

4. Ann wants a state flag from all the states. She has some flags. How many more flags does she need? 10

PROBLEM SOLVING PRACTICE

Solve each problem. Draw a picture if needed.

1. Steve had 7 stamps from Italy. He got 6 more. How many stamps from Italy does he have all together? 13

2. A large envelope is 9 inches long. A small envelope is 5 inches long. How much longer is a large envelope? 4 inches

3. John's mother sent him 9 letters while he was away. One got lost in the mail. How many letters did John receive?

4. Mary had 5 large envelopes and 6 small envelopes. How many envelopes did she have in all? 11

5. Jack had $8. He spent $3 for stamps. How much money did he have left? $5

6. Beverly received 3 letters on Monday and 6 on Tuesday. How many did she receive in all? 9

Read each problem. Would you *add* or *subtract*?

★**7.** Carmen had ▲ stamps. She put ● stamps on her letters. How many stamps does she have left? 3

★**8.** While he was at camp, Thomas wrote ▲ letters to his family and ● letters to his friends. How many letters did Thomas write? 5

Fact Families

A. You could write four addition and subtraction facts after looking at this domino.

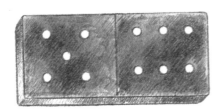

$5 + 6 = 11$
$6 + 5 = 11$
$11 - 6 = 5$
$11 - 5 = 6$

These four facts are called a **fact family**.

B. Domino pictures can also help you find **missing addends.** Suppose you know that there are 7 dots on this domino. How many dots are covered?

$4 + \blacksquare = 7$ 4 plus what is 7?
$4 + 3 = 7$
3 is the answer.

If there are 7 dots in all, how many dots are covered?

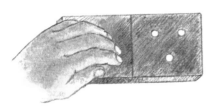

$\blacksquare + 3 = 7$ What plus 3 is 7?
$4 + 3 = 7$
4 is the answer.

TRY THESE

Find the sums and differences in each fact family.

1. $8 + 5 = \boxed{13}$
   $5 + 8 = \boxed{13}$
   $13 - 5 = \boxed{8}$
   $13 - 8 = \boxed{5}$

2. $14 - 9 = \boxed{5}$
   $14 - 5 = \boxed{9}$
   $9 + 5 = \boxed{14}$
   $5 + 9 = \boxed{14}$

3. $4 + 7 = \boxed{11}$
   $11 - 7 = \boxed{4}$
   $7 + 4 = \boxed{11}$
   $11 - 4 = \boxed{7}$

Find the missing addends.

4. $5 + \boxed{2} = 7$

5. $8 + \boxed{8} = 16$

6. $\boxed{2} + 4 = 6$

SKILLS PRACTICE _____

Find the sums and differences in each fact family.

1. $9 + 6 = $ ■ 15
   $6 + 9 = $ ■ 15
   $15 - 9 = $ ■ 6
   $15 - 6 = $ ■ 9

2. $14 - 8 = $ ■ 6
   $14 - 6 = $ ■ 8
   $8 + 6 = $ ■ 14
   $6 + 8 = $ ■ 14

3. $7 + 5 = $ ■ 12
   $12 - 5 = $ ■ 7
   $5 + 7 = $ ■ 12
   $12 - 7 = $ ■ 5

Find the missing addends.

4. $9 + $ 2 $ = 11$

5. $7 + $ 8 $ = 15$

6. 7 $ + 9 = 16$

7. 4 $ + 7 = 11$

8. $9 + $ 2 $ = 11$

9. $8 + $ 6 $ = 14$

10. $8 + $ 4 $ = 12$

11. 0 $ + 4 = 4$

12. $8 + $ 2 $ = 10$

13. $5 + $ 0 $ = 5$

14. 3 $ + 5 = 8$

15. $5 + $ 3 $ = 8$

16. $9 + $ 0 $ = 9$

17. 5 $ + 6 = 11$

★18. 0 $ + $ 0 $ = 0$

19. The two addends are 9 and 8.
    Write the members of this fact family.

20. The two addends are 0 and 2.
    Write the members of this fact family.

★21. Each addend is 8.
    Write the members of this fact family.

★22. Each addend is 0.
    Write the members of this fact family.

★23. What is the missing sign in this fact?
    $4 \bullet 3 = 7$

✓ Unit Checkup

Add to find the sums. *(pages 2–3)*

1. 5
+6
11

2. 8
+8
16

3. 3
+8
11

4. 5
+9
14

5. 9
+8
17

6. 6
+6
12

7. 5
+8
13

8. 4
+7
11

9. 7
+4
11

10. 0
+9
9

11. 8
+9
17

12. 7
+6
13

13. 6
+7
13

14. 7
+0
7

15. 9
+7
16

16. 6
+8
14

17. 5
+5
10

18. 4
+9
13

19. 5
+7
12

20. 8
+5
13

21. 7
+7
14

22. 4
5
+4
13

23. 8
0
+1
9

24. 3
2
+5
10

25. 6
3
+1
10

26. 2
4
+3
9

27. 4
4
+4
12

28. 5
3
+4
12

Complete the number sentences. *(pages 4–5)*

29. 6 + 9 = 15

30. 8 + 4 = 12

31. 9 + 2 = 11

32. 2 + 4 = 6

33. 0 + 4 = 4

34. 3 + 6 + 3 = 12

Subtract to find the differences. *(pages 10–11)*

35. 15
− 6
9

36. 13
− 9
4

37. 12
− 5
7

38. 7
−2
5

39. 14
− 9
5

40. 17
− 8
9

41. 11
− 3
8

42. 6
−6
0

43. 7
−0
7

44. 12
− 4
8

45. 18
− 9
9

46. 2
−0
2

47. 10
− 7
3

48. 1
−1
0

49. 13
− 7
6

50. 10
− 9
1

51. 17
− 9
8

52. 11
− 4
7

53. 11
− 8
3

54. 13
− 5
6

55. 15
− 8
7

Complete the number sentences. *(pages 12–13)*

56. 12 − 9 = 3

57. 14 − 5 = 9

58. 8 − 8 = 0

59. 16 − 8 = 8

60. 5 − 0 = 5

61. 11 − 6 = 5

20   **Reviewing Addition and Subtraction Facts**

Add or subtract. *(pages 2-3, 10-11)*

62. 13
− 8
___
5

63. 7
+8
___
15

64. 8
+7
___
15

65. 14
− 6
___
8

66. 11
− 7
___
4

67. 9
+6
___
15

68. 7
+9
___
16

69. 9
+3
___
12

70. 11
− 9
___
2

71. 16
− 7
___
9

72. 12
− 6
___
6

73. 7
+8
___
15

74. 9
+9
___
18

75. 3
+7
___
10

76. 15
− 9
___
6

77. 9
+4
___
13

78. 12
− 7
___
5

79. 4
+8
___
12

80. 16
− 9
___
7

81. 8
+6
___
14

82. 15
− 7
___
8

Find the sums and differences in each fact family. *(pages 18-19)*

83. 8 + 2 = ■ 10
2 + 8 = ■ 10
10 − 8 = ■ 2
10 − 2 = ■ 8

84. 13 − 7 = ■ 6
13 − 6 = ■ 7
6 + 7 = ■ 13
7 + 6 = ■ 13

85. 3 + 9 = ■ 12
12 − 3 = ■ 9
9 + 3 = ■ 12
12 − 9 = ■ 3

Find the missing addends. *(pages 18-19)*

86. 3 + ■ = 11   8

87. 4 + ■ = 13   9

88. ■ + 8 = 15   7

89. ■ + 7 = 14   7

90. 9 + ■ = 18   9

91. 6 + ■ = 10   4

Solve the problems. Draw pictures if needed. *(pages 6-7, 14-17)*

92. The flag of the United States has 7 red stripes and 6 white stripes. How many stripes does it have in all? 13

93. The city flag of Detroit has 13 stars. The city flag of Chicago has 4 stars. How many more stars does the Detroit flag have? 9

94. Raoul drew the state flag of Alaska with 8 stars. He drew the state flag of Tennessee with 3 stars. How many stars did he draw? 11

95. The state flag of Rhode Island has 13 stars. The state flag of Alaska has 8 stars. How many more stars does the Rhode Island flag have? 5

96. Diane had 18 state flags. She gave 9 of them to Paul. How many flags does she have left? 9

97. Eric had 8 state flags. His sister sent him 6 more flags. How many flags did Eric have then? 14

21

Reinforcement

More Help with Addition

$$\begin{array}{r} 4 \\ +5 \\ \hline 9 \end{array}$$

$$\begin{array}{r} 5 \\ +0 \\ \hline 5 \end{array}$$

$$\begin{array}{r} 3 \\ 4 \\ +3 \\ \hline 10 \end{array} \Big\} 7 \qquad \begin{array}{r} 3 \\ +3 \\ \hline 10 \end{array} \qquad \begin{array}{r} 3 \\ 4 \\ +3 \\ \hline 10 \end{array} \Big\} \begin{array}{r} 3 \\ +7 \\ \hline 10 \end{array}$$

Add.

1. $\begin{array}{r} 5 \\ +8 \\ \hline 13 \end{array}$
2. $\begin{array}{r} 6 \\ +5 \\ \hline 11 \end{array}$
3. $\begin{array}{r} 3 \\ +9 \\ \hline 12 \end{array}$
4. $\begin{array}{r} 7 \\ +8 \\ \hline 15 \end{array}$

5. $\begin{array}{r} 0 \\ +7 \\ \hline 7 \end{array}$
6. $\begin{array}{r} 7 \\ +9 \\ \hline 16 \end{array}$
7. $\begin{array}{r} 8 \\ +6 \\ \hline 14 \end{array}$
8. $\begin{array}{r} 8 \\ +9 \\ \hline 17 \end{array}$

9. $\begin{array}{r} 7 \\ +5 \\ \hline 12 \end{array}$
10. $\begin{array}{r} 9 \\ +5 \\ \hline 14 \end{array}$
11. $\begin{array}{r} 2 \\ +9 \\ \hline 11 \end{array}$
12. $\begin{array}{r} 8 \\ +0 \\ \hline 8 \end{array}$

13. $\begin{array}{r} 5 \\ 2 \\ +1 \\ \hline 8 \end{array}$
14. $\begin{array}{r} 4 \\ 4 \\ +2 \\ \hline 10 \end{array}$
15. $\begin{array}{r} 6 \\ 2 \\ +3 \\ \hline 11 \end{array}$
16. $\begin{array}{r} 5 \\ 3 \\ +4 \\ \hline 12 \end{array}$

More Help with Subtraction

$$\begin{array}{r} 5 \\ -3 \\ \hline 2 \end{array}$$

$$\begin{array}{r} 3 \\ -3 \\ \hline 0 \end{array}$$

$$\begin{array}{r} 4 \\ -0 \\ \hline 4 \end{array}$$

Subtract.

17. $\begin{array}{r} 12 \\ -\ 8 \\ \hline 4 \end{array}$
18. $\begin{array}{r} 16 \\ -\ 9 \\ \hline 7 \end{array}$
19. $\begin{array}{r} 13 \\ -\ 8 \\ \hline 5 \end{array}$
20. $\begin{array}{r} 11 \\ -\ 2 \\ \hline 9 \end{array}$

21. $\begin{array}{r} 11 \\ -\ 5 \\ \hline 6 \end{array}$
22. $\begin{array}{r} 17 \\ -\ 8 \\ \hline 9 \end{array}$
23. $\begin{array}{r} 10 \\ -\ 6 \\ \hline 4 \end{array}$
24. $\begin{array}{r} 15 \\ -\ 7 \\ \hline 8 \end{array}$

25. $\begin{array}{r} 9 \\ -0 \\ \hline 9 \end{array}$
26. $\begin{array}{r} 13 \\ -\ 6 \\ \hline 7 \end{array}$
27. $\begin{array}{r} 13 \\ -\ 4 \\ \hline 9 \end{array}$
28. $\begin{array}{r} 7 \\ -7 \\ \hline 0 \end{array}$

29. $\begin{array}{r} 14 \\ -\ 8 \\ \hline 6 \end{array}$
30. $\begin{array}{r} 17 \\ -\ 9 \\ \hline 8 \end{array}$
31. $\begin{array}{r} 12 \\ -\ 3 \\ \hline 9 \end{array}$
32. $\begin{array}{r} 14 \\ -\ 7 \\ \hline 7 \end{array}$

Grouping with Parentheses and Brackets

( ) are parentheses.
Parentheses group numbers.
Work inside the parentheses first.

$$8 - \overset{\lceil\ 3\ \rceil}{(2 + 1)} = 5 \qquad (8 - 2) \overset{\lceil\ 6\ \rceil}{+ 1} = 7$$

1. $8 - (4 - 3) = $ ▨ 7

2. $(8 - 4) - 3 = $ ▨ 1

3. $8 + (4 - 3) = $ ▨ 9

4. $(8 + 4) - 3 = $ ▨ 9

[ ] are brackets.
When parentheses and brackets are used,
work inside the parentheses first and
then work inside the brackets.

$$[(9 - 6) + 4] - 1 = 6 \qquad 9 - [6 + (4 - 1)] = 0$$

5. $[9 - (5 - 3)] + 2 = $ ▨ 9

6. $[(9 - 5) - 3] + 2 = $ ▨ 3

7. $[4 + (8 - 3)] + 4 = $ ▨ 13

8. $[(4 + 8) - 3] + 4 = $ ▨ 13

9. $8 - [6 - (4 + 1)] = $ ▨ 7

10. $[8 - (6 - 4)] + 1 = $ ▨ 7

Copy each exercise. Place parentheses to show how the answer was found.

11. $(8 - 4) + 3 = 7$

12. $8 - (4 + 3) = 1$

Copy each exercise. Place parentheses and brackets to show how the answer was found.

13. $[(17 - 9) + 5] - 6 = 7$

14. $17 - [(9 + 5) - 6] = 9$

14

8

23

Maintaining Skills

Choose the correct answer.

1. 9
  +6

a. 3
b. 15
c. 14
d. not above

2. 13
  − 8

a. 6
b. 4
c. 15
d. not above

3. 12
  − 5

a. 3
b. 7
c. 9
d. not above

4. 8
  +4

a. 4
b. 12
c. 14
d. not above

5. 7
  +9

a. 16
b. 17
c. 12
d. not above

6. 9
  −3

a. 12
b. 4
c. 6
d. not above

7. $7 + 4 = $ ▩

a. 11
b. 3
c. 10
d. not above

8. $6 + $ ▩ $ = 9$

a. 6
b. 15
c. 8
d. not above

9. $7 - 0 = $ ▩

a. 7
b. 17
c. 0
d. not above

10. $6 - 6 = $ ▩

a. 3
b. 6
c. 12
d. not above

11. 3
  2
  +6

a. 5
b. 12
c. 11
d. not above

12. $4 + 3 + 5 = $ ▩

a. 7
b. 8
c. 12
d. not above

13. Sandy took 9 pictures at the park. Pat took 7 pictures. How many pictures did they take?

a. 2 pictures
b. 16 pictures
c. 17 pictures
d. not above

14. Rosa took 6 pictures at home and 9 pictures at school. How many more pictures did she take at school?

a. 15 pictures
b. 17 pictures
c. 16 pictures
d. not above

Hundreds

| 2 hundreds | 7 tens | 5 ones |

Hundreds	Tens	Ones
2	7	5

275 is a
standard numeral.

The digit 2 in the **hundreds place** means 2 hundreds.

The digit 7 in the **tens place** means 7 tens.

The digit 5 in the **ones place** means 5 ones.

Write: 275   **Read:** two hundred seventy-five

TRY THESE

Write the standard numerals.

1.   74

2.   205

3. Name the place of the digit 7 in the standard numeral 716.

4. Give the meaning of the digit 6 in the standard numeral 600.

5. Write the standard numeral for three hundred ten. 310

6. Show how to read 349.
3 hundreds
4 tens
9 ones

7. Show how to read 801.
8 hundreds
0 tens
1 one

26   **Place Value**

SKILLS PRACTICE

Write the standard numerals.

1.

2.

3. eight hundred fifty-seven

4. six hundred eighteen

5. seven hundred six

6. five hundred forty

For each standard numeral name the place of the digit 9.

7. 915   8. 695   9. 29   10. 900   11. 90   12. 309

For each standard numeral give the meaning of the digit 8.

13. 187   14. 308   15. 380   16. 82   17. 800   18. 823

Match.

19. 52   a. five hundred twelve
20. 520   b. five hundred two
21. 502   c. fifty-two
22. 512   d. five hundred twenty

Show how to read each standard numeral.

23. 340   24. 200

25. 952   26. 402

Use the three digits to write all of the three-digit numerals you can.

27. 2, 5, 8   ★28. 4, 7, 7   ★29. 3, 3, 3

30. A teller at the bank had 3 rolls of 100 pennies, 2 stacks of 10 pennies, and 8 extra pennies. How many pennies did she have?

★31. Another teller had 587 pennies. How many full rolls of 100 pennies could he make?

Comparing Whole Numbers

A. This **number line** shows the order of whole numbers. The whole numbers are in order from **least** to **greatest**.

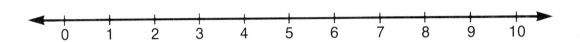

B. A number line can help you **compare** numbers.

> < means *less than*
> > means *greater than*

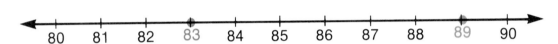

83 is to the left of 89.
83 is less than 89.
83 < 89

89 is to the right of 83.
89 is greater than 83.
89 > 83

C.

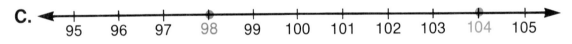

98 is to the left of 104.
98 is less than 104.
98 < 104

104 is to the right of 98.
104 is greater than 98.
104 > 98

The symbol always points to the smaller number!

TRY THESE

Compare. Write one statement using < and one statement using > for each exercise.

1. 24
    19

2. 36
    42

3. 109
    99

4. 527
    537

5. 759
    761

Write >, <, or = for ●.

1. 49 ● 52
2. 47 ● 41
3. 55 ● 55
4. 88 ● 98
5. 73 ● 69
6. 82 ● 88
7. 76 ● 67
8. 89 ● 91
9. 99 ● 101
10. 109 ● 109
11. 523 ● 515
12. 567 ● 561
13. 323 ● 325
14. 709 ● 711
15. 436 ● 426
16. 468 ● 460
17. 829 ● 829
18. 999 ● 998

PROBLEM SOLVING

The ticket taker at the state fair must keep certain kinds of records.
Copy and complete these records.

19.

Attendance	
Sat.	482
Sun.	478
Day with greater attendance:	

20.

Hours Worked	
Sat.	9
Sun.	7
Total	

21.

Booths at Fair	
Open	14
Closed	6
How many more open?	

EXTRA! Using a Pattern

Find the missing numbers.

A. 487, ■, 489, ■, 491, 492, ■, 494

B. 97, 98, ■, ■, 101, 102, ■, 104, 105

C. 60, ■, 80, 90, ■, ■, 120

Ms. Ellen Riley
Oak St.
Treetown, Me.

Rounding Numbers

You can **round** the numbers to tell about how many.

A. Round the numbers in red to the **nearest ten.**

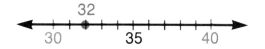

32 is nearer 30 than 40.
32 rounds down to 30.

167 is nearer 170 than 160.
167 rounds up to 170.

85 is as near 80 as 90.
Round 85 up to 90.

> When a number is exactly in the middle, round up.

B. Round to the **nearest hundred** or **nearest dollar.**

328 is nearer 300 than 400.
328 rounds down to 300.

$6.50 is as near $6.00 as $7.00.
Round $6.50 up to $7.00.

TRY THESE

Round to the nearest ten.

1. 38   **2.** 35   **3.** 169   **4.** 161   **5.** 82   **6.** 84

Round to the nearest hundred or nearest dollar.

7. 390   **8.** 350   **9.** 302   **10.** $6.98   **11.** $6.45   **12.** $6.75

SKILLS PRACTICE

Round to the nearest ten. Use the number line if you need help.

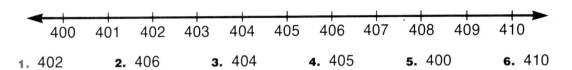

1. 402　　2. 406　　3. 404　　4. 405　　5. 400　　6. 410

Round to the nearest hundred. Use the number line if you need help.

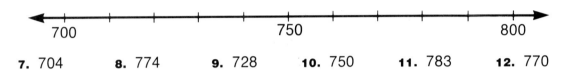

7. 704　　8. 774　　9. 728　　10. 750　　11. 783　　12. 770

Round to the nearest dollar. Use the number line if needed.

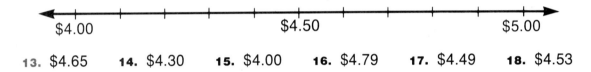

13. $4.65　　14. $4.30　　15. $4.00　　16. $4.79　　17. $4.49　　18. $4.53

Round to the nearest ten. Use the number line if needed.

19. 43　　20. 543　　21. 402　　22. 575　　★23. 296　　★24. 98

Round to the nearest hundred or nearest dollar.

25. 678　　26. $2.45　　27. 439　　28. 198　　29. $4.96　　★30. $.99

Round each number to the nearest ten and to the nearest hundred.

31. 442　　32. 250　　33. 117　　34. 487　　★35. 983　　★36. 347

PROBLEM SOLVING

37. Round each temperature to the nearest ten.

★38. Which city had the highest temperature? Which had the lowest?

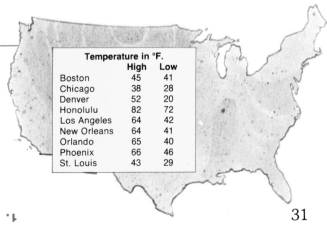

Temperature in °F.		
	High	Low
Boston	45	41
Chicago	38	28
Denver	52	20
Honolulu	82	72
Los Angeles	64	42
New Orleans	64	41
Orlando	65	40
Phoenix	66	46
St. Louis	43	29

ⓐ Maintaining Skills

Add.

1. $\begin{array}{r} 2 \\ +4 \\ \hline \end{array}$	2. $\begin{array}{r} 6 \\ +3 \\ \hline \end{array}$	3. $\begin{array}{r} 3 \\ +9 \\ \hline \end{array}$	4. $\begin{array}{r} 4 \\ +7 \\ \hline \end{array}$	5. $\begin{array}{r} 0 \\ +8 \\ \hline \end{array}$	6. $\begin{array}{r} 9 \\ +7 \\ \hline \end{array}$	7. $\begin{array}{r} 6 \\ +6 \\ \hline \end{array}$
8. $\begin{array}{r} 3 \\ +5 \\ \hline \end{array}$	9. $\begin{array}{r} 4 \\ +9 \\ \hline \end{array}$	10. $\begin{array}{r} 6 \\ +8 \\ \hline \end{array}$	11. $\begin{array}{r} 7 \\ +2 \\ \hline \end{array}$	12. $\begin{array}{r} 5 \\ +6 \\ \hline \end{array}$	13. $\begin{array}{r} 8 \\ +4 \\ \hline \end{array}$	14. $\begin{array}{r} 7 \\ +3 \\ \hline \end{array}$

15. $5 + 7 = $ ▨   16. $9 + 9 = $ ▨   17. $8 + 7 = $ ▨

Subtract.

18. $\begin{array}{r} 9 \\ -2 \\ \hline \end{array}$	19. $\begin{array}{r} 15 \\ -7 \\ \hline \end{array}$	20. $\begin{array}{r} 5 \\ -4 \\ \hline \end{array}$	21. $\begin{array}{r} 10 \\ -6 \\ \hline \end{array}$	22. $\begin{array}{r} 9 \\ -3 \\ \hline \end{array}$	23. $\begin{array}{r} 7 \\ -3 \\ \hline \end{array}$	24. $\begin{array}{r} 8 \\ -6 \\ \hline \end{array}$
25. $\begin{array}{r} 12 \\ -6 \\ \hline \end{array}$	26. $\begin{array}{r} 10 \\ -8 \\ \hline \end{array}$	27. $\begin{array}{r} 11 \\ -4 \\ \hline \end{array}$	28. $\begin{array}{r} 14 \\ -5 \\ \hline \end{array}$	29. $\begin{array}{r} 12 \\ -7 \\ \hline \end{array}$	30. $\begin{array}{r} 14 \\ -8 \\ \hline \end{array}$	31. $\begin{array}{r} 17 \\ -9 \\ \hline \end{array}$

32. $9 - 7 = $ ▨   33. $16 - 8 = $ ▨   34. $8 - 8 = $ ▨

Add or subtract.

35. $\begin{array}{r} 6 \\ +1 \\ \hline \end{array}$	36. $\begin{array}{r} 17 \\ -8 \\ \hline \end{array}$	37. $\begin{array}{r} 2 \\ +8 \\ \hline \end{array}$	38. $\begin{array}{r} 9 \\ +5 \\ \hline \end{array}$	39. $\begin{array}{r} 10 \\ -4 \\ \hline \end{array}$	40. $\begin{array}{r} 12 \\ -9 \\ \hline \end{array}$	41. $\begin{array}{r} 8 \\ +8 \\ \hline \end{array}$
42. $\begin{array}{r} 11 \\ -7 \\ \hline \end{array}$	43. $\begin{array}{r} 4 \\ +6 \\ \hline \end{array}$	44. $\begin{array}{r} 7 \\ -5 \\ \hline \end{array}$	45. $\begin{array}{r} 3 \\ +3 \\ \hline \end{array}$	46. $\begin{array}{r} 13 \\ -8 \\ \hline \end{array}$	47. $\begin{array}{r} 15 \\ -9 \\ \hline \end{array}$	48. $\begin{array}{r} 9 \\ +8 \\ \hline \end{array}$

49. $9 + 6 = $ ▨   50. $13 - 4 = $ ▨   51. $5 + 8 = $ ▨

Solve the problems.

52. Lisa had 8 records. She bought 2 more records. How many records did she have?

53. Brad had 14 records. He let Joan borrow 6 records. How many records did he have left?

Project: Organizing Information

Here is a record of traffic that passed by a school one morning. The crossing guard made a mark / in her chart each time a vehicle drove by. When she had 4 marks ////, she showed the fifth mark like this ////. This is called **tallying.** Later, she counted the marks to get the totals.

Type	Tally	Total
bus	//// /	6
car	//// //// //// ////	20
motorcycle	//// ///	8
taxi	////	4
truck	//// //// //// //	17

1. Copy and complete this **bar graph** to show the information in the chart. Color one square for each vehicle. The bar for bus is done for you.

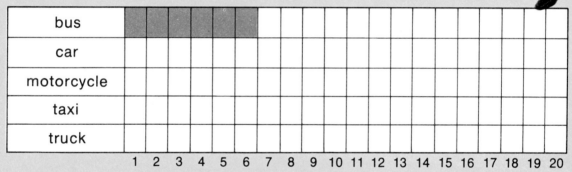

bus	
car	
motorcycle	
taxi	
truck	

1 2 3 4 5 6 7 8 9 10 11 12 13 14 15 16 17 18 19 20

Write the total for each set of tally marks.

2. //// ||

3. //// //// ||

4. //// //// //// //// |

Make tally marks to show each number.

5. 24

6. 9

7. 32

Ask each of your classmates or your neighbors to name his or her favorite sport. Make a tally record and bar graph to show your results.

Think of some other information which you would like to collect. Make a tally record and bar graph for that information.

Thousands

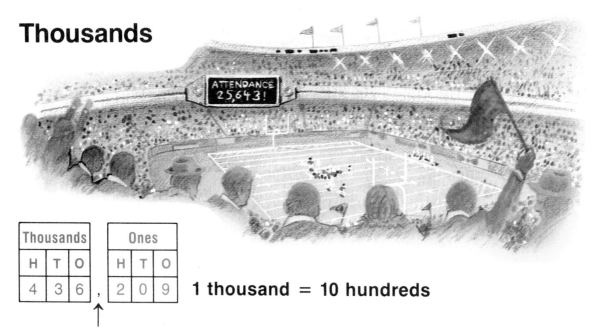

Thousands			Ones		
H	T	O	H	T	O
4	3	6	2	0	9

1 thousand = 10 hundreds

A comma separates the **ones period** and the **thousands period.**

4 in the **hundred-thousands place** means 4 hundred-thousands.

3 in the **ten-thousands place** means 3 ten-thousands.
6 in the **thousands place** means 6 thousands.

Write: 436,209
Read: four hundred thirty-six thousand two hundred nine.

TRY THESE

For each standard numeral name the place of the digit 2.

1. 2,711
2. 758,208
3. 420,377
4. 219,875

5. What does each digit mean in 520,930?

Write the standard numerals.

6. three hundred eighty-four thousand six hundred nineteen

7. seventy thousand seventy
8. four hundred thousand four

Show how to read the standard numerals.

9. 900,300
10. 21,008
11. 650,000

For each standard numeral name the place of the digit 6.

1. 68,483   2. 690,954   3. 1,964   4. 43,605

For each standard numeral give the meaning of the digit 5.

5. 5,678   6. 50,432   7. 100,500   8. 500,010

Write the standard numerals.

9. three thousand seventy-six

10. twenty-nine thousand four hundred fifty

11. three hundred thousand three

12. two hundred eighteen thousand seven hundred twelve

13. seventy-four thousand forty

14. seven hundred forty thousand four

Show how to read each standard numeral.

15. 20,020   16. 390,200   17. 9,010   18. 800,001

19. Write the standard numeral with digits that mean 8 ten-thousands 6 thousands 4 hundreds 9 tens 3 ones.

★20. Write the standard numeral with 7 in the hundred-thousands place, 5 in the thousands place, 3 in the tens place and zeros in all other places.

Use the four digits to write the smallest and the largest four-digit standard numeral.

★21. 2, 9, 0, 1   ★22. 5, 2, 7, 3   ★23. 1, 6, 1, 6   ★24. 4, 0, 8, 0

Comparing Larger Numbers

A. If the numbers you are comparing do not have the same number of digits, the number with more digits is greater.

Compare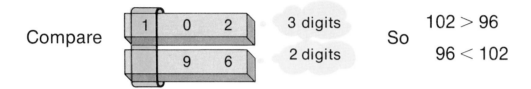

3 digits	102 > 96
2 digits	96 < 102

So

B. If the numbers you are comparing have the same number of digits, look at the digits on the left.

Compare

| 2, | 8 | 4 | 9 |
| 5, | 0 | 3 | 6 |

2 < 5
5 > 2

So

2,849 < 5,036
5,036 > 2,849

C. If the digits on the left are the same, look to the right until you find digits that are different.

Compare

| 3 | 9, | 5 | 8 | 4 |
| 3 | 9, | 5 | 6 | 1 |

8 > 6
6 < 8

So

39,584 > 39,561
39,561 < 39,584

D. If all the digits are the same, the numbers are equal.

342,987 = 342,987

TRY THESE

Compare. Write one statement using > and one statement using < for each exercise.

1. 1,023
   989

2. 6,003
   5,942

3. 837
  847

4. 69,015
   69,072

SKILLS PRACTICE

Write >, <, or = for ⬤.

1. 93 ⬤ 527
2. 703 ⬤ 298
3. 4,286 ⬤ 4,531
4. 23,198 ⬤ 23,501
5. 3,692 ⬤ 3,692
6. 13,384 ⬤ 9,254
7. 14,037 ⬤ 14,039
8. 130,492 ⬤ 99,687
9. 417,120 ⬤ 415,890
10. 20,316 ⬤ 20,316
11. 827,431 ⬤ 827,426
12. 168,300 ⬤ 168,301

Write the larger number.

★ 13. eight thousand forty-seven
80,047

★ 14. forty thousand twenty-three
40,032

PROBLEM SOLVING

15. The *Queen Elizabeth 2* and the *Norway* are passenger ships. The *Queen Elizabeth 2* is 289 meters long. The *Norway* is 311 meters long. Which ship is longer?

16. The *Queen Elizabeth 2* can carry 60,167 metric tons. The *Norway* can carry 59,713 metric tons. Which ship can carry more?

17. The sailing distance from New York to Bermuda is 1,283 kilometers. The sailing distance from New York to the Grand Bahama Island is 1,769 kilometers. Which island is farther from New York?

18. The sailing distance from San Francisco to Anchorage, Alaska, is 3,445 kilometers. The sailing distance from San Francisco to Acapulco, Mexico, is 3,373 kilometers. Which city is farther from San Francisco?

EXTRA! Comparing Values
Think about the sums or differences.
Write >, <, or = for ⬤.

A. $2 + 3$ ⬤ 10
B. $6 + 8$ ⬤ 12
C. 14 ⬤ $7 + 7$
D. $16 - 9$ ⬤ 8
E. $12 - 4$ ⬤ 8
F. 7 ⬤ $13 - 5$

Millions

About 250,000,000 red blood cells die and are replaced in each person every day.

A.

Millions			Thousands			Ones		
H	T	O	H	T	O	H	T	O
2	4	8	3	5	0	1	6	9

2 | 4 | 8 , 3 | 5 | 0 , 1 | 6 | 9

↑   ↑

1 million = 10 hundred-thousands

Commas separate the ones, thousands, and millions periods.

2 in the **hundred-millions place** means 2 hundred-millions.
4 in the **ten-millions place** means 4 ten-millions.
8 in the **millions place** means 8 millions.

Write: 248,350,169   **Read:** two hundred forty-eight million three hundred fifty thousand one hundred sixty-nine

B. You can compare millions as you did thousands.

Compare   8 9,0 7 2,5 1 6   5 > 4   So   89,072,516 > 89,072,498
         8 9,0 7 2,4 9 8   4 < 5   89,072,498 < 89,072,516

TRY THESE

For each standard numeral name the place of the digit 3.

1. 43,802,057   **2.** 138,642,500   **3.** 9,437,159   **4.** 300,000,000

For each standard numeral give the meaning of the digit 6.

5. 264,521,312   **6.** 5,069,847   **7.** 610,720,000   **8.** 26,015,942

9. Write the standard numeral for ten million five-hundred fifty.

10. Show how to read the standard numeral 503,005,000.

Compare. Use > and < to write two statements.

11. 3,458,207
     3,547,207

12. 100,500,000
     105,000,000

13. 27,098,000
     27,908,000

SKILLS PRACTICE

For each standard numeral name the place of the digit 9.

1. 903,477,688   2. 93,000,028   3. 2,908,617   4. 9,726,400

For each standard numeral give the meaning of the digit 5.

5. 25,002,101   6. 573,101,000   7. 50,700,000   8. 528,234

Write the standard numerals.

9. six hundred forty-two million three hundred thousand sixty

10. seventy million four hundred eighty thousand two hundred

11. nine hundred million nine hundred thousand nine hundred

Match.

12. five hundred forty million   a. 504,000,000

13. five hundred four million   b. 5,004,000

14. five million four thousand   c. 540,000,000

Show how to read each standard numeral.

15. 6,006,006   16. 798,000,000   17. 10,500,006   18. 40,040,000

Write > , <, or = for ●.

19. 13,544,275 ● 13,455,275   20. 207,000,000 ● 270,000,000

21. 5,000,000 ● 4,999,999   22. 3,000,000 ● 998,277

PROBLEM SOLVING

Most Active Stocks	
Sales	**Company**
484,000	P & R OIL
579,000	AIR FLEET
398,000	GENERAL PAPER

E&M
$3 MILLION
SALE

GREENS
$700
THOUSAND
SALE

23. Which stock was the most active (had the most sales)?

★24. Which store had the larger sale?

Problem Solving: Too Much Information

A table shows a large amount of information. You must read carefully to select only the information you need to solve each problem.

READ   PLAN   DO   ANSWER   CHECK

AIR DISTANCE IN KILOMETERS (km) BETWEEN CITIES OF THE WORLD

	Athens	Berlin	Chicago	Hong Kong	London
Athens		1,807	8,764	8,546	2,416
Berlin	1,807		7,084	8,851	924
Chicago	8,764	7,084		12,537	6,357
Hong Kong	8,546	8,851	12,537		9,625
London	2,416	924	6,357	9,625	

To find the distance between Chicago and Athens, you can look down ↓ to Chicago and across → to Athens. The distance is 8,764 kilometers. You can also look across → to Chicago and down ↓ to Athens. The distance is the same.

TRY THESE

1. How far apart are Athens and London?

2. How far apart are Berlin and London?

3. Which two cities in the table are farthest apart?

4. Find the distance between Athens and Hong Kong.

5. Find the distance between Chicago and London.

6. Write two statements using < and > to compare the distance between Athens and Hong Kong and between Chicago and London.

7. Round the distance between Berlin and Athens to the nearest ten. Then round it to the nearest hundred.

PROBLEM SOLVING PRACTICE

Use this table to solve the problems below.

DRIVING DISTANCE IN KILOMETERS BETWEEN CITIES OF THE U.S.	Atlanta	Dallas	Denver	Jacksonville	Los Angeles	Philadelphia
Atlanta, GA		1,309	2,405	521	3,632	1,260
Dallas, TX	1,309		1,287	1,647	2,322	2,473
Denver, CO	2,405	1,287		2,879	2,035	2,755
Jacksonville, FL	521	1,647	2,879		3,970	1,445
Los Angeles, CA	3,632	2,322	2,035	3,970		4,543
Philadelphia, PA	1,260	2,473	2,755	1,445	4,543	

1. In November, a football team traveled by bus from Atlanta to Jacksonville. Was the distance the team traveled greater than 500 kilometers?

2. The Greene family drove from Denver to Jacksonville. The Sanchez family drove from Los Angeles to Atlanta. Which family drove farther?

3. On their vacation, Rob and his father drove from Dallas to Philadelphia. What was the distance they traveled?

4. A tour bus started its tour in Dallas and drove to Denver. What was the distance it traveled?

5. Which 2 cities are the farthest apart?

6. Which 2 cities are closest together?

7. Round the distance between Philadelphia and Dallas to the nearest ten. Then round it to the nearest hundred.

★ 8. How many pairs of cities that are listed in this table are farther than 3,500 kilometers apart?

✓ Unit Checkup

For each standard numeral name the place of the digit 5.
(pages 26–27, 34–35)

1. 5,948
2. 50,672
3. 8,500

For each standard numeral give the meaning of the digit 4.
(pages 26–27, 34–35, 38–39)

4. 487
5. 8,426
6. 453,907

7. 242,709
8. 34,206
9. 24,397,005

Show how to read each standard numeral. *(pages 34–35, 38–39)*

10. 6,439
11. 181,521

12. 32,289
13. 49,366

14. 407,090
15. 19,000,300

Write the numerals. *(pages 34–35, 38–39)*

16. four thousand two hundred fifty-seven
17. thirty-two thousand six hundred three
18. sixty-seven thousand forty-two
19. nine thousand three hundred eighty-one
20. five hundred four thousand ninety-one
21. eight million forty-seven

Write >, <, or = for ●. *(pages 28–29, 36–37)*

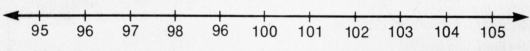

22. 96 ● 98
23. 101 ● 97
24. 103 ● 103

25. 243 ● 89
26. 896 ● 901
27. 7,869 ● 7,870

28. 11,101 ● 11,124
29. 201,021 ● 201,021
30. 998,021 ● 997,986

Round each number to the nearest ten. *(pages 30–31)*

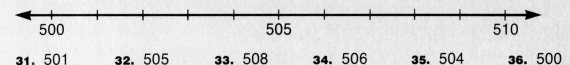

31. 501   **32.** 505   **33.** 508   **34.** 506   **35.** 504   **36.** 500

Round each number to the nearest hundred. *(pages 30–31)*

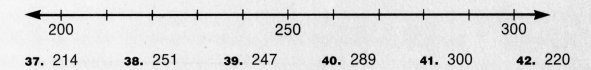

37. 214   **38.** 251   **39.** 247   **40.** 289   **41.** 300   **42.** 220

Round each amount to the nearest dollar. *(pages 30–31)*

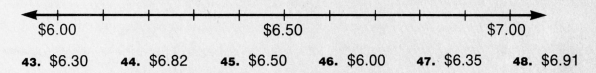

43. $6.30   **44.** $6.82   **45.** $6.50   **46.** $6.00   **47.** $6.35   **48.** $6.91

Use the table to solve the following problems. *(pages 40–41)*

DRIVING DISTANCE IN KILOMETERS BETWEEN CITIES OF THE U.S.

	Boston	Houston	St. Louis	San Francisco
Boston, MA		3,066	1,885	5,061
Houston, TX	3,066		1,270	3,128
St. Louis, MO	1,885	1,270		3,402
San Francisco, CA	5,061	3,128	3,402	

49. A truck delivering new washing machines traveled from St. Louis to San Francisco. What was the distance the truck traveled?

50. A truck transporting automobile parts traveled from Houston to Boston. Was the distance traveled greater than 1,000 kilometers?

51. A truck traveled from San Francisco to St. Louis. A bus traveled from San Francisco to Houston. Which traveled farther?

52. There are four cities in the table. Which two cities are the closest together?

⌐Reinforcement

More Help with Place Value

Thousands			Ones		
H	T	O	H	T	O
9	5	1	8	1	0

(951,810)

The digit 5 is in the ten-thousands place. The digit 5 means 5 ten-thousands.

For each standard numeral name the place of the digit 5.

1. 15,902

2. 62,542

3. 50,008

4. 571,373

For each standard numeral give the meaning of the digit 5.

5. 71,587

6. 533,624

7. 25,209

8. 156,487

Write:
503,062

Read:
five hundred three thousand sixty-two

Write the numerals.

9. four thousand ninety-two

10. sixty-three thousand five

11. three hundred fifty-eight thousand fifty-seven

Show how to read each standard numeral.

12. 290,382

13. 305,002

14. 7,640

15. 136,000

16. 10,101

17. 57,659

More Help with Rounding

573
nearest ten 570
nearest hundred 600

Round each number to the nearest ten and nearest hundred.

18. 472

19. 321

20. 543

21. 485

22. 796

23. 659

Roman Numerals

The Romans used letters to name numbers. This is how they wrote the numerals for 1 through 10.

To write 4, they put I before V to mean subtract 1 from 5.

To write 9, they put I before X to mean subtract 1 from 10.

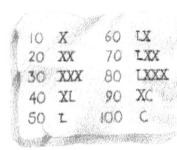

This is how they wrote the numerals to count by tens.

To write 40, they put X before L to mean subtract 10 from 50.

To write 90, they put X before C to mean subtract 10 from 100.

Notice that the Romans never wrote any letter more than three times in a row. Study these Roman numerals.

10 + 3	20 + 9	40 + 5	60 + 7	90 + 4
XIII	XXIX	XLV	LXVII	XCIV

What number does each Roman numeral name?

1. VII
2. XVI
3. XXII
4. XIV

5. XL
6. LVII
7. LXVIII
8. XCI

Write the Roman numeral for each.

9. 12
10. 24
11. 42
12. 69

13. 53
14. 75
15. 88
16. 94

b Maintaining Skills

Choose the correct answer.

1.
$$\begin{array}{r} 9 \\ +5 \\ \hline \end{array}$$
a. 14
b. 15
c. 4
d. not given

2.
$$\begin{array}{r} 16 \\ -\ 7 \\ \hline \end{array}$$
a. 11
b. 8
c. 9
d. not given

3. $7 - 7 =$
a. 0
b. 14
c. 7
d. not given

4. $5 + 6 =$
a. 10
b. 13
c. 12
d. not given

5. $3 + = 9$
a. 6
b. 12
c. 7
d. not given

6. $4 + 3 + 2 =$
a. 5
b. 7
c. 8
d. not given

7. What does the digit 8 mean in 8,479?
a. 8 thousands
b. 8 hundreds
c. 8 ones
d. not given

8. Find thirteen thousand eight.
a. 13,000,008
b. 130,008
c. 13,080
d. not given

9. 988 1,476
a. >
b. <
c. =

10. 5,629 5,634
a. >
b. <
c. =

11. Round 275 to the nearest ten.
a. 300
b. 270
c. 280
d. not given

12. Round 687 to the nearest hundred.
a. 690
b. 700
c. 600
d. not given

13. Mount Shasta is 14,162 ft high. Mount Evans is 14,262 ft high. Which one is higher?
a. Mount Evans
c. Mount Shasta
b. both the same
d. not given

14. Susan paid $8.45 for a new scarf. How much did she pay to the nearest dollar?
a. $9.00
c. $8.00
b. $8.50
d. not given

Addition and Subtraction 3

Adding 2-digit Numbers

A. There are 36 bicycles with baskets.
There are 42 bicycles without baskets.
How many bicycles are there in all?

You can add to find how many bicycles in all.

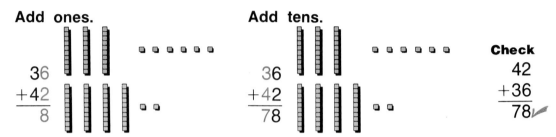

Add ones.

```
 36
+42
  8
```

Add tens.

```
 36
+42
 78
```

Check

```
 42
+36
 78✓
```

There are 78 bicycles.

B. Sometimes you must regroup 10 ones as 1 ten.

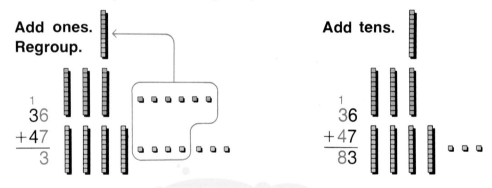

Add ones.
Regroup.

```
  1
 36
+47
  3
```

Add tens.

```
  1
 36
+47
 83
```

13 ones is 1 ten 3 ones.

TRY THESE _____

Add. Check your answers.

1.
```
 32
+21
```
2.
```
 75
+24
```
3.
```
 51
+ 3
```
4.
```
 27
+36
```
5.
```
 63
+ 9
```
6.
```
 49
+39
```

7. $82 + 14 = $ ▨

8. $75 + 13 = $ ▨

9. $22 + 9 = $ ▨

SKILLS PRACTICE

Add.

1. 73 +16	**2.** 60 +25	**3.** 6 +43	**4.** 48 +33	**5.** 44 +22	**6.** 15 +76
7. 15 +78	**8.** 27 +62	**9.** 29 +22	**10.** 1 +45	**11.** 25 + 4	**12.** 13 +68
13. 27 +57	**14.** 53 +39	**15.** 37 +14	**16.** 36 +25	**17.** 25 +42	**18.** 32 +39
19. 71 +19	**20.** 46 +42	**21.** 67 +13	**22.** 48 +26	**23.** 58 +23	**24.** 7 +42
25. 62 +26	**26.** 75 +18	**27.** 19 +25	**28.** 49 +30	**29.** 63 +28	**30.** 43 +49

31. $30 + 50 = $ ▧

32. $74 + 8 = $ ▧

33. $15 + 80 = $ ▧

34. $32 + 48 = $ ▧

35. $6 + 37 = $ ▧

36. $28 + 55 = $ ▧

PROBLEM SOLVING

37. Mr. Samuels sold 74 racing bikes. He sold 24 children's bikes. How many bikes did he sell in all?

38. Mrs. Samuels ordered 17 racing bikes and 9 other bikes. How many more racing bikes did she order?

39. Town and Country Bike Shop sold 47 bikes in April. In May they sold 35 bikes. How many bikes did they sell all together?

40. Larry spent $79 for a bike. He spent $8 for a light for the bike. How much did he spend in all?

★ **41.** There were 18 bikes in a bike rack. Lisa and her 2 brothers put their bikes in the rack. How many bikes were in the rack then?

★ **42.** Jack rode 25 kilometers on Saturday and 32 kilometers on Sunday. How many kilometers did he ride in all?

Larger Sums

A. Sometimes you must regroup 10 tens as 1 hundred.

Add ones.   **Add tens.**
                                               Regroup.

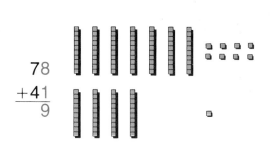
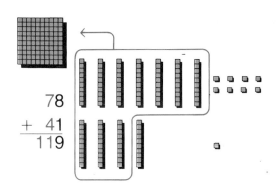

78
+41
 9

78
+ 41
119

B. 78 + 57 = ▦

Add ones.   ¹78
           +57
             5

Add tens.   ¹78
           +57
           135

15 ones is 1 ten 5 ones.   13 tens is 1 hundred 3 tens.

TRY THESE _____

Add. Check your answers.

1. 46	2. 87	3. 95	4. 89	5. 8	6. 53
+81	+22	+43	+84	+96	+78

7. 21 + 87 = ▦   **8.** 94 + 6 = ▦   **9.** 44 + 96 = ▦

50   **Addition and Subtraction**

SKILLS PRACTICE

Add.

1. $\begin{array}{r} 75 \\ +41 \\ \hline \end{array}$ 2. $\begin{array}{r} 36 \\ +\ 2 \\ \hline \end{array}$ 3. $\begin{array}{r} 84 \\ +15 \\ \hline \end{array}$ 4. $\begin{array}{r} 99 \\ +32 \\ \hline \end{array}$ 5. $\begin{array}{r} 18 \\ +90 \\ \hline \end{array}$ 6. $\begin{array}{r} 64 \\ +23 \\ \hline \end{array}$

7. $\begin{array}{r} 45 \\ +74 \\ \hline \end{array}$ 8. $\begin{array}{r} 83 \\ +88 \\ \hline \end{array}$ 9. $\begin{array}{r} 30 \\ +97 \\ \hline \end{array}$ 10. $\begin{array}{r} 76 \\ +25 \\ \hline \end{array}$ 11. $\begin{array}{r} 56 \\ +\ 5 \\ \hline \end{array}$ 12. $\begin{array}{r} 64 \\ +68 \\ \hline \end{array}$

13. $\begin{array}{r} 35 \\ +86 \\ \hline \end{array}$ 14. $\begin{array}{r} 74 \\ +67 \\ \hline \end{array}$ 15. $\begin{array}{r} 85 \\ +\ 7 \\ \hline \end{array}$ 16. $\begin{array}{r} 29 \\ +75 \\ \hline \end{array}$ 17. $\begin{array}{r} 35 \\ +13 \\ \hline \end{array}$ 18. $\begin{array}{r} 71 \\ +\ 9 \\ \hline \end{array}$

19. $\begin{array}{r} 66 \\ +74 \\ \hline \end{array}$ 20. $\begin{array}{r} 35 \\ +55 \\ \hline \end{array}$ 21. $\begin{array}{r} 3 \\ +38 \\ \hline \end{array}$ 22. $\begin{array}{r} 29 \\ +84 \\ \hline \end{array}$ 23. $\begin{array}{r} 62 \\ +37 \\ \hline \end{array}$ 24. $\begin{array}{r} 57 \\ +99 \\ \hline \end{array}$

25. $80 + 10 = $ ▨   26. $47 + 9 = $ ▨   27. $46 + 19 = $ ▨

28. $28 + 79 = $ ▨   29. $9 + 94 = $ ▨   30. $18 + 36 = $ ▨

PROBLEM SOLVING

31. Charlie had 45 records in one case and 32 records in another case. How many records did he have?

32. Mike bought 12 records last year and 19 records this year. When did he buy more records?

★ 33. Gail danced to 2 records. The first record was 27 minutes long and the second was 25 minutes long. How long did she dance?

★ 34. David had 89 records. His brother borrowed 17 records and his sister borrowed 15. How many records did they borrow all together?

A clerk at a music store kept the following records. Copy and complete them.

	Bought	Sold	On hand
Feb. 28			17
35. Mar. 1	0	9	▨
36. Mar. 2	4	0	▨
★ 37. Mar. 3	3	6	▨

CASH	
On hand	$15
Spent	$6
38. Left	▨
Earned	$10
39. On hand	▨

Adding 3-digit Numbers

A. The school store sold 382 ball-point pens and 407 felt-tip pens. How many pens were sold in all?

Add ones.	382 $+407$	Add tens.	382 $+407$	Add hundreds.	382 $+407$
	9		89		789

789 pens were sold.

B. Sometimes you must regroup.

Add ones.

$$\begin{array}{r}\overset{1}{9}87\\+495\\\hline2\end{array}$$

Add tens.

$$\begin{array}{r}\overset{1\,1}{9}87\\+495\\\hline82\end{array}$$

Add hundreds.

$$\begin{array}{r}\overset{1\,1}{9}87\\+495\\\hline1,482\end{array}$$

14 hundreds is 1 thousand 4 hundreds.

C. To add dollars and cents, you can think of the number of cents.

$$\begin{array}{r}\$4.26\\+\ 7.53\\\hline\end{array}$$

$4.26 = 426¢
$7.53 = 753¢

$$\begin{array}{r}426¢\\+753¢\\\hline1179¢\end{array}$$

so

$$\begin{array}{r}\$4.26\\+\ 7.53\\\hline\$11.79\end{array}$$

TRY THESE

Add. Check your answers.

1. $\begin{array}{r}234\\+145\\\hline\end{array}$

2. $\begin{array}{r}728\\+\ 46\\\hline\end{array}$

3. $\begin{array}{r}445\\+263\\\hline\end{array}$

4. $\begin{array}{r}84\\+619\\\hline\end{array}$

5. $\begin{array}{r}\$9.20\\+\ 7.86\\\hline\end{array}$

6. $\begin{array}{r}\$4.79\\+\ 6.82\\\hline\end{array}$

7. $308 + 70 = $ ▓

8. $8 + 993 = $ ▓

9. $\$6.89 + \$4.73 = $ ▓

SKILLS PRACTICE _____

Add.

1. 586
    + 12

2. 538
    +641

3. 823
    +145

4. 46
    +57

5. 683
    +748

6. 774
    +869

7. 704
    +519

8. 996
    + 7

9. 857
    +174

10. 409
    +693

11. 813
    +288

12. 69
    +32

13. 237
    +765

14. 274
    +705

15. 9
    +894

16. 543
    +678

17. 936
    + 68

18. 249
    +453

19. 19
    +88

20. 967
    +950

21. 327
    +753

22. 807
    + 95

23. 784
    +205

24. 93
    +418

25. 984
    +836

26. 185
    +658

27. 37
    +98

28. $7.93
    + 1.59

29. $3.80
    + 6.25

30. $6.57
    + 2.98

31. 84 + 917 =

32. 369 + 842 =

33. 723 + 186 =

34. 3 + 997 =

35. 56 + 49 =

36. $6.37 + $8.76 =

PROBLEM SOLVING _____

37. The school store sold 49 three-ring notebooks and 239 spiral notebooks. How many notebooks were sold in all?

38. Fred bought a pen for $1.99 and crayons for $2.79. How much money did he spend?

The school store kept a notebook that showed what was sold. Some of the pages were ripped. Find the missing numbers.

★ 39.
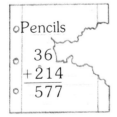

```
 Pencils
    36
  +214
   577
```

★ 40.
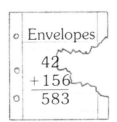

```
 Envelopes
    42
  +156
   583
```

★ 41.

```
 Folders
    5 7
  +23
   754
```

Workbook   page 402

53

Adding 4-digit Numbers

You can add thousands just as you add hundreds, tens, and ones. You may need to regroup many times.

5,623 tickets were sold on Saturday.
7,198 tickets were sold on Sunday.
How many tickets were sold in all?

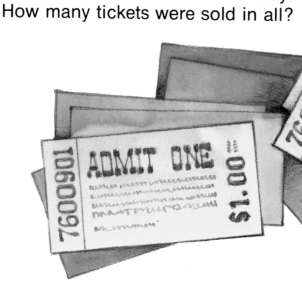

Add ones.	Add tens.	Add hundreds.	Add thousands.
1	1 1	1 1	1 1
5,623	5,623	5,623	5,623
+7,198	+7,198	+7,198	+7,198
1	21	821	12,821

12,821 tickets were sold.

> 12 thousands is
> 1 ten-thousand 2 thousands

TRY THESE

Add. Check your answers.

1. 2,471
    +   26

2. 6,543
    + 725

3. 7,045
    +3,216

4. 8,362
    +4,189

5. $59.63
    + 96.89

6. 3,902 + 816 = ▧

7. 4,238 + 6,097 = ▧

8. $37.99 + $37.99 = ▧

SKILLS PRACTICE

Add.

1. 5,862
   +3,107

2. 4,781
   +6,542

3. 876
   +543

4. 1,792
   + 349

5. 6,186
   +9,295

6. 8,723
   +8,599

7. 99
   +316

8. 3,214
   +2,043

9. 7,819
   +8,749

10. 5,306
    +9,186

11. 2,455
    +9,657

12. 486
    +7,878

13. 9,999
    +9,999

14. 560
    +972

15. 1,495
    +3,627

16. 7,459
    +9,862

17. 3,294
    +7,764

18. 802
    + 49

19. 9,008
    + 999

20. 79
    +79

21. 2,536
    +4,061

22. 8,139
    +9,269

23. $46.99
    + 57.82

24. $59.75
    + 72.36

25. $ .36
    + 18.97

26. 730 + 8,612 = ■

27. 3,462 + 1,828 = ■

28. 7,525 + 75 = ■

29. 5,462 + 9,307 = ■

30. 6,457 + 6,975 = ■

31. $32.14 + $60.71 = ■

PROBLEM SOLVING

32. 7,642 people bought tickets before the ball game. 876 people bought tickets at the game. How many people in all bought tickets?

33. There were 1,232 hits made in a stadium in one year. 1,579 hits were made in the next year. How many hits were made in all?

★ 34. 9,285 people arrived at the stadium before the game. 312 people arrived during the first 15 minutes of the game. How many people in all were at the stadium 15 minutes after the game started?

★ 35. 1,200 people sat in Section 1 of the stadium. 1,991 people sat in Section 2 of the stadium. In which section were more people sitting?

Rounding to Any Place

A. To round to the **nearest hundred**, circle the **hundreds digit.** Look at the digit to its right.

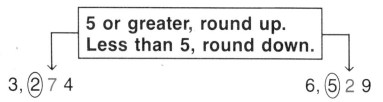

| 5 or greater, round up. |
| Less than 5, round down. |

3,②7 4   6,⑤2 9

7 > 5   **Round up.**   2 < 5   **Round down.**

To round up: **To round down:**

Add 1 to the hundreds digit.   Keep the hundreds digit.
Write 0's to the right.   Write 0's to the right.

$$\begin{array}{r} 3,②7\ 4 \\ +\quad\ 1 \\ \hline 3,3\,0\ 0 \end{array}$$

$$\begin{array}{r} 6,⑤2\ 9 \\ \downarrow \\ \hline 6,5\,0\ 0 \end{array}$$

B. To round to the **nearest thousand**, circle the **thousands digit.** Look at the digit to its right.

⑥, 5 2 9   ③, 2 7 4

5   Add 1.   2 < 5   Keep ③.

$$\begin{array}{r} ⑥,\,5\ 2\ 9 \\ +1 \\ \hline 7,\,0\ 0\ 0 \end{array}$$

$$\begin{array}{r} ③,\,2\ 7\ 4 \\ \downarrow \\ \hline 3,\,0\ 0\ 0 \end{array}$$

C. Round 32,998 to the **nearest ten.** To the **nearest ten-thousand.**

Nearest ten.   **Nearest ten-thousand.**

$$\begin{array}{r} 3\,2,9⑨\,8 \\ +\qquad 1 \\ \hline 3\,3,0\,0 \end{array}$$ 8 > 5
Add 1.

$$\begin{array}{r} ③\,2,9\ 9\ 8 \\ \downarrow \\ \hline 3\,0,0\ 0\ 0 \end{array}$$ 2 < 5
Keep ③.

TRY THESE

Round to the nearest ten.

1. 48   **2.** 65   **3.** 151   **4.** 392   **5.** 4,297   **6.** 8,995

Round to the nearest hundred.

7. 191   **8.** 236   **9.** 987   **10.** 1,326   **11.** 13,500   **12.** 48,972

Round to the nearest thousand.

13. 7,246   **14.** 3,506   **15.** 9,978   **16.** 21,635   **17.** 342,500

SKILLS PRACTICE

Round to the nearest ten.

1. 37   **2.** 75   **3.** 99   **4.** 491   **5.** 6,197   **6.** 12,694

Round to the nearest hundred.

7. 751   **8.** 600   **9.** 942   **10.** 9,998   **11.** 91,239   **12.** 66,500

Round to the nearest thousand.

13. 7,486   **14.** 3,602   **15.** 9,979   **16.** 425,800   **17.** 999,850

Round to the nearest ten-thousand.

18. 52,545   **19.** 25,100   **20.** 40,000   **21.** 263,900   **22.** 998,172

What digits could you use in place of the ▮ to make each statement true?

★ **23.** 2,▮46 rounded to the nearest thousand is 2,000.

★ **24.** 2,▮46 rounded to the nearest thousand is 3,000.

Estimating Sums

An **estimate** of a sum is a number that is easy to find *and* is near the exact sum.

A. To estimate a sum use three steps.

1. Find the smaller number. Circle its first digit. Circle the digit in the same place in the other number.

$$\begin{array}{r} ⑤47 \\ +2{,}③86 \\ \hline \end{array}$$

2. Round both numbers to the circled place.

$$\begin{array}{rcl} ⑤47 & \rightarrow & 500 \\ +2{,}③86 & \rightarrow & 2{,}400 \\ \hline \end{array}$$

3. Add the rounded numbers to get the estimate.

$$\begin{array}{r} 500 \\ +2{,}400 \\ \hline 2{,}900 \end{array}$$

2,900 is an estimate of 547 + 2,386.

B. You can use estimation to check an addition to see if your answer is reasonable.

Exact sum

$$\begin{array}{r} \overset{1\ 1}{} \\ \$54.32 \\ +\ 9.87 \\ \hline \$64.19 \end{array}$$

Estimate

$$\begin{array}{rcl} \$5④.32 & \rightarrow & \$54.00 \\ +\ ⑨.87 & \rightarrow & 10.00 \\ \hline & & \$64.00 \end{array}$$

$64.19 is near $64.00. The answer is reasonable.

TRY THESE _____

Find each sum. Then estimate to check your sum.

1.
$$\begin{array}{r} 573 \\ +3{,}246 \\ \hline \end{array}$$

2.
$$\begin{array}{r} 862 \\ +519 \\ \hline \end{array}$$

3.
$$\begin{array}{r} 923 \\ +5{,}416 \\ \hline \end{array}$$

4.
$$\begin{array}{r} 8{,}563 \\ +8{,}465 \\ \hline \end{array}$$

5.
$$\begin{array}{r} 2{,}690 \\ +\ \ 478 \\ \hline \end{array}$$

SKILLS PRACTICE

Find each sum. Then estimate to check your sum.

1. 739
 +203

2. 847
 +436

3. 6,234
 +5,722

4. 1,276
 + 439

5. 2,541
 + 983

6. 5,297
 +3,862

7. 9,823
 +8,032

8. 7,692
 + 560

9. 4,734
 + 886

10. 8,067
 +9,083

11. 3,862
 +4,976

12. 7,043
 +8,962

13. 5,687
 + 496

14. 6,098
 + 887

15. 979
 +6,190

16. 7,854 + 6,902 = ■

17. 864 + 3,298 = ■

18. 8,938 + 956 = ■

19. 8,793 + 436 = ■

20. 6,794 + 8,203 = ■

21. 2,148 + 876 = ■

PROBLEM SOLVING

★ 22. Estimate the sum of 3,245 and 1,246. Do you think the estimate is greater than or less than the exact sum?

★ 23. Estimate the sum of 3,972 and 983. Do you think the estimate is greater than or less than the exact sum?

EXTRA! Making Logical Choices

A visitor to the planet Oog was greeted by 1 Foog and 2 Toogs. The visitor knew that Foogs always make false statements and that Toogs always tell the truth. Each greeter made one statement:

A said, "B is a Foog." B said, "I am a Toog." C said, "I am not a Foog."

Which of the three can the visitor be *sure* is a Toog?

Adding 5-digit Numbers

A. When you add large numbers, you may have to regroup many times.

88,796 copies of the *Miami News* were sold on Monday morning. 8,448 copies were sold on Monday afternoon. How many copies were sold in all?

Ones	Tens	Hundreds	Thousands	Ten-thousands
1	1 1	1 1 1	1 1 1 1	1 1 1 1
88,796	88,796	88,796	88,796	88,796
+ 8,448	+ 8,448	+ 8,448	+ 8,448	+ 8,448
4	44	244	7,244	97,244

97,244 copies were sold.

B. You can check your addition by estimating.

$$
\begin{array}{rcr}
88,796 & \longrightarrow & 89,000 \\
+\ 8,448 & \longrightarrow & +\ 8,000 \\
\hline
97,244 & & 97,000
\end{array}
$$

97,244 is near 97,000.
The answer is reasonable.

TRY THESE

Add. Check your answers by estimating.

	1.	2.	3.	4.	5.
	24,627	8,594	48,681	70,973	47,936
	+57,081	+ 967	+30,947	+29,126	+ 8,497

6. 22,389 + 56,724 = ▨   **7.** 643 + 18,298 = ▨   **8.** 47,285 + 1,238 = ▨

SKILLS PRACTICE

Add.

1. 28,570
+ 7,660

2. 67,527
+28,605

3. 32,879
+96,151

4. 27,385
+83,927

5. 33,695
+54,105

6. 86,435
+67,842

7. 86,300
+79,251

8. 71,558
+28,442

9. 7,865
+39,326

10. 90,000
+80,000

11. 56,421
+32,069

12. 82,906
+18,287

13. 69,169
+ 5,871

14. 978
+27,455

15. 78,414
+ 9,841

16. 52,749
+ 6,478

17. 7,348
+26,819

18. 19,989
+23,976

19. $805.63
+ 194.37

20. $964.50
+ 28.49

21. 60,805 + 4,257 = ▓

22. 50,000 + 70,000 = ▓

23. 71,475 + 985 = ▓

24. $97.30 + $498.50 = ▓

Find the missing digits.

★ 25. 4,724
+ ▓,836
8,560

★ 26. 9,274
+6,▓▓7
15,461

★ 27. 14,▓6▓
+ 2,5▓7
17,159

PROBLEM SOLVING

28. 52,553 copies of the *Jacksonville Journal* were sold last Saturday. 52,533 copies were sold this Saturday. On which Saturday were more copies sold?

29. 94,237 copies of the *Sacramento Union* were sold on Saturday. 95,683 copies were sold on Sunday. How many copies were sold on the weekend?

30. One store in Denver sold 819 copies of the *Denver Post* in a week. Another store sold 1,629 copies. How many newspapers were sold in all?

31. Kenny delivers 2,379 copies of the *Denver Post* each month. Peter delivers 2,183 copies each month. How many copies do they deliver in all?

Adding More Than Two Numbers

A. When you add more than two numbers, you may
regroup to form two or more tens or hundreds.

Add ones.

$$
\begin{array}{r}
\overset{2}{7}9 \\
63 \\
+98 \\
\hline
0
\end{array}
\qquad
\begin{array}{r}
9 \\
+3 \\
\hline
12 \\
+\ 8 \\
\hline
20
\end{array}
$$

$$
\begin{array}{r}
\overset{2}{7}9 \\
63 \\
+98 \\
\hline
240
\end{array}
\qquad
\begin{array}{r}
2 \\
+7 \\
\hline
9 \\
+6 \\
\hline
15 \\
+\ 9 \\
\hline
24
\end{array}
$$

Add tens.

B. You can add larger numbers the same way.
Use estimation to check.

$$
\begin{array}{rcl}
\overset{1\ 2\ 3\ 3}{\textcircled{3},498} & \longrightarrow & 3,000 \\
6\textcircled{2},799 & \longrightarrow & 63,000 \\
\textcircled{1},689 & \longrightarrow & 2,000 \\
+1\textcircled{5},519 & \longrightarrow & +16,000 \\
\hline
83,505 & & 84,000
\end{array}
$$

83,505 is near 84,000 ✓

TRY THESE _____

Add. Check your answers by estimating.

1.	2.	3.	4.	5.	6.
8	21	304	393	79,630	9,987
9	35	219	13,846	18,471	618
+8	+47	+846	+18,773	46,800	4,786
				+22,562	+4,467

7. 56,718 + 629 + 298 + 308 = ▩

8. 2,148 + 193 + 184 + 60,365 = ▩

Add.

1.   9
    4
  +7

2.   58
   79
 +86

3.   478
  859
+674

4. $93.00
  78.50
+ 75.00

5. $348.72
  16.97
+ 248.33

6.   7
   8
   5
  +6

7.   49
  99
  75
 +86

8.   387
   71
 569
+878

9. 1,389
  965
1,201
+   98

10. 14,379
  5,685
17,388
+21,477

11.   3
   6
   7
   2
  +4

12.   27
    8
  14
  32
 +29

13.   300
   28
 472
 189
+ 76

14. 1,600
2,800
3,400
+5,500

15. 23,757
68,291
 4,147
+35,793

16. $7,832 + 479 + 6,042 = $ ▨

17. $9,999 + 6,200 + 6,870 = $ ▨

18. $16,583 + 77,324 + 14,385 = $ ▨

19. $\$379.22 + \$48.95 + \$37.68 = $ ▨

PROBLEM SOLVING

20. In one month, 61,772 airplanes landed at Chicago's O'Hare Airport. 43,046 planes landed at the Atlanta Airport and 35,808 planes landed at the airport in Phoenix. How many planes landed at these airports that month?

21. The air distance between San Francisco and Tokyo is 8,240 km. The distance between Tokyo and Paris is 9,685 km. Is the distance between San Francisco and Tokyo greater than or less than the distance between Tokyo and Paris?

★ 22. 3,427 people boarded planes through Gate 1. 2,877 people boarded planes through Gate 2. 9,766 people boarded through Gate 3. How many people boarded through these three gates?

★ 23. In June of 1977, 22,666 planes landed at Boston's Logan Airport. 27,535 planes landed in July, and 31,642 landed in August. How many planes landed in these 3 months?

 Maintaining Skills

Add or subtract.

1. 13 − 5	**2.** 6 +7	**3.** 12 − 9	**4.** 8 +7	**5.** 14 − 8	**6.** 11 − 6	**7.** 7 +9
8. 16 − 7	**9.** 9 +7	**10.** 15 − 9	**11.** 9 +8	**12.** 17 − 9	**13.** 8 +6	**14.** 17 − 8
15. 14 − 5	**16.** 8 +8	**17.** 13 − 7	**18.** 6 +9	**19.** 9 +5	**20.** 15 − 6	**21.** 9 +9

Write the standard numerals.

22. seventy-two thousand one hundred thirty-nine

23. six hundred ninety thousand two hundred sixteen

24. eight thousand four

25. fourteen thousand five hundred

For each standard numeral name the place of the digit 4.

26. 47,025

27. 200,174

28. 408,030

Show how to read each standard numeral.

29. 8,190

30. 20,060

31. 150,000

For each standard numeral give the meaning of the digit 7.

32. 670,019

33. 5,678

34. 715,608

35. 437,589

Round to the nearest hundred.

36. 876

37. 750

38. 437

39. 857

40. 389

Solve the problems.

41. The home team hit 8 home runs. The visiting team hit 9 home runs. How many home runs were hit in all?

42. There are 16 sections in the ball park. 9 sections are full. How many sections are not full?

64   **Addition and Subtraction**

Project: Writing Instructions

You can easily carry out the instruction:

List "temperature" and "stand" in alphabetical order.

It is not so easy to tell someone how to list two words in alphabetical order. You must be able to write, in order, a set of step-by-step instructions. Such a set of instructions is called an **algorithm**.

An example of an algorithm is given below. It is written in language that people can understand. When an algorithm is written in language that a **computer** can understand, it is called a **program**.

> **To use an algorithm complete the steps in the numbered order unless a step tells you to go to another step.**

To list two words in alphabetical order you can follow these steps:

Step 1. Look at the first letter of each word.
Step 2. Compare the letters. If they are different, go to **Step 6.**
Step 3. If one word has no next letter, go to **Step 7.**
Step 4. Look at the next letter of each word.
Step 5. Go to **Step 2.**
Step 6. List the words in the order in which the letters you just compared appear in the alphabet. Stop!
Step 7. List the word with no next letter before the other word. Stop!

To list "temperature" and "stand" in alphabetical order these steps of the algorithm would be used:

1., 2., 6.

To list "stand" and "still" in alphabetical order these steps of the algorithm would be used:

1., 2., 3., 4., 5., 2., 3., 4., 5., 2., 6.

Write the steps that would be used to list each pair of words in alphabetical order.

1. dog, cat   **2.** in, inside   **3.** stand, state
4. I, it   **5.** out, ouch   **6.** of, off

Subtracting 2-digit Numbers

A. 64 people were on the bus.
At Hill Street, 23 people
got off. How many people
were left on the bus?

You can subtract to find how many people were left.

Subtract ones.　　　**Subtract tens.**　　　**Check**

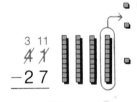

$$\begin{array}{r} 64 \\ -23 \\ \hline 1 \end{array} \qquad \begin{array}{r} 64 \\ -23 \\ \hline 41 \end{array} \qquad \begin{array}{r} 41 \\ +23 \\ \hline 64 \end{array}$$

41 people were left on the bus.

B. Sometimes you must regroup before you
can subtract.

Regroup.　　　**Subtract ones.**　　　**Subtract tens.**

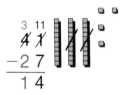

$$\begin{array}{r} {\scriptstyle 3\ 11} \\ \cancel{4}\ \cancel{1} \\ -2\ 7 \\ \hline \end{array} \qquad \begin{array}{r} {\scriptstyle 3\ 11} \\ \cancel{4}\ \cancel{1} \\ -2\ 7 \\ \hline 4 \end{array} \qquad \begin{array}{r} {\scriptstyle 3\ 11} \\ \cancel{4}\ \cancel{1} \\ -2\ 7 \\ \hline 1\ 4 \end{array}$$

4 tens 1 one is 3 tens 11 ones.

TRY THESE

Subtract. Use addition to check.

1.　$\begin{array}{r} 57 \\ -25 \\ \hline \end{array}$　　**2.**　$\begin{array}{r} 69 \\ -63 \\ \hline \end{array}$　　**3.**　$\begin{array}{r} 75 \\ -\ 3 \\ \hline \end{array}$　　**4.**　$\begin{array}{r} 42 \\ -17 \\ \hline \end{array}$　　**5.**　$\begin{array}{r} 35 \\ -\ 9 \\ \hline \end{array}$　　**6.**　$\begin{array}{r} 83 \\ -79 \\ \hline \end{array}$

7. $79 - 46 = $ ■　　　　**8.** $47 - 8 = $ ■　　　　**9.** $67 - 59 = $ ■

SKILLS PRACTICE

Subtract.

1. 68 −13	2. 76 −30	3. 38 −13	4. 42 − 8	5. 70 −18	6. 51 −38
7. 77 − 7	8. 34 −28	9. 82 −65	10. 60 − 3	11. 33 − 6	12. 48 −29
13. 29 −24	14. 37 −21	15. 84 −17	16. 55 −24	17. 86 −52	18. 58 − 7

19. 93 − 85 = ▧   20. 50 − 7 = ▧   21. 68 − 15 = ▧

22. 75 − 37 = ▧   23. 67 − 60 = ▧   24. 90 − 47 = ▧

Add or subtract.

25. 90 −34	26. 45 −36	27. 61 −49	28. 68 +27	29. 76 +49	30. 48 −40
31. 52 −26	32. 96 +78	33. 91 − 4	34. 63 +38	35. 46 −46	36. 93 −15

PROBLEM SOLVING

37. Mr. Bates had $75. He spent $22 for a bus ticket. How much money did he have left?

38. 38 students were on the school bus. 25 more students got on at Ridge Ave. How many students were on the bus then?

★ 39. 48 people were on the bus. At the first stop, 23 people got off. How many people were on the bus then? After the 23 people got off, 17 people got on. How many people were on the bus then?

★ 40. At the first stop, 46 people got on the bus. At the next stop, 19 people got off and 4 got on. At the next stop, 12 got off and 10 got on. At the last stop, 29 people got off. How many stops did the bus make?

Subtracting 3-digit Numbers

293
~~539~~
SALE
GUPPIES

A. The owner of a tropical fish
   store had 539 guppies.
   She sold 246 guppies.
   How many guppies were left?

| Subtract ones. | $\begin{array}{r} 539 \\ -246 \\ \hline 3 \end{array}$ | Regroup. Subtract tens. | $\begin{array}{r} {}^{4\ 13}\ \\ 5\ 3\ 9 \\ -2\ 4\ 6 \\ \hline 9\ 3 \end{array}$ | Subtract hundreds. | $\begin{array}{r} {}^{4\ 13}\ \\ 5\ 3\ 9 \\ -2\ 4\ 6 \\ \hline 2\ 9\ 3 \end{array}$ |

293 guppies were left.

B. 851 − 683 = ▨

| Regroup. Subtract ones. | $\begin{array}{r} {}^{4\ 11}\ \\ 8\ 5\ 1 \\ -6\ 8\ 3 \\ \hline 8 \end{array}$ | Regroup. Subtract tens. | $\begin{array}{r} {}^{7\ 4\ 11}\ \\ 8\ 5\ 1 \\ -6\ 8\ 3 \\ \hline 6\ 8 \end{array}$ | Subtract hundreds. | $\begin{array}{r} {}^{7\ 4\ 11}\ \\ 8\ 5\ 1 \\ -6\ 8\ 3 \\ \hline 1\ 6\ 8 \end{array}$ |

C. To subtract dollars and cents, think of
   the number of cents.

| $\begin{array}{r} \$5.62 \\ -\ 2.49 \\ \hline \end{array}$ | $5.62 = 562¢$ $2.49 = 249¢$ | $\begin{array}{r} {}^{5\ 12}\ \\ 562¢ \\ -249¢ \\ \hline 313¢ \end{array}$ | SO | $\begin{array}{r} {}^{5\ 12}\ \\ \$5.62 \\ -\ 2.49 \\ \hline \$3.13 \end{array}$ |

TRY THESE

Subtract. Use addition to check.

1. $\begin{array}{r} 925 \\ -603 \\ \hline \end{array}$ **2.** $\begin{array}{r} 583 \\ -149 \\ \hline \end{array}$ **3.** $\begin{array}{r} 437 \\ -\ 64 \\ \hline \end{array}$ **4.** $\begin{array}{r} 782 \\ -736 \\ \hline \end{array}$ **5.** $\begin{array}{r} 864 \\ -\ 97 \\ \hline \end{array}$ **6.** $\begin{array}{r} \$7.25 \\ -\ 4.99 \\ \hline \end{array}$

7. 610 − 38 = ▨   **8.** $7.33 − $1.88 = ▨   **9.** 471 − 386 = ▨

SKILLS PRACTICE

Subtract.

1. 758 −623	2. 480 −120	3. 562 −124	4. 849 −762	5. 482 − 67	6. 870 −258
7. 519 −347	8. 405 − 23	9. 608 −597	10. 562 −253	11. 682 −498	12. 95 −87
13. 273 − 69	14. 361 −169	15. 648 − 93	16. 572 −279	17. $5.53 − 3.75	18. $3.26 − .89

19. $968 - 289 = $ ▨   20. $426 - 302 = $ ▨   21. $314 - 16 = $ ▨

22. $239 - 37 = $ ▨   23. $109 - 5 = $ ▨   24. $3.07 - $1.43 = ▨

PROBLEM SOLVING

25. Sue had $9.50. She spent $7.99 for a fish tank. How much money did she have left?

26. Jeff has 146 tropical fish. Carlos has 138 tropical fish. How many fish do they have?

★ 27. A large fish tank contains 147 liters of water and 27 fish. The tank holds 732 liters of water when it is full. How many more liters are needed to fill the tank?

★ 28. Ken put 47 goldfish in one tank and 52 goldfish in another tank. How many goldfish were in the tanks? Ken sold 12 of the goldfish. How many goldfish were left?

Keep a record of the number of fish in the tank.

		Record
Start with 38.		38
29. Buy	246	▨
30. Sell	51	▨
31. Sell	110	▨
32. Buy	78	▨

George worked part time at the pet store. Keep a record of the money he spent and earned.

		Record
Start with $6.75		$6.75
33. Spend	$1.25	▨
34. Earn	$3.75	▨
35. Spend	$4.89	▨
36. Earn	$2.50	▨

Zeros in Subtraction

Sometimes you must regroup both hundreds and tens before you can subtract the ones.

A. The students in Ms. Adler's class collected 204 rocks. They painted 86 of them. How many rocks were not painted?

Regroup hundreds.
$$\begin{array}{r} 1\ 10\\ \not{2}\not{0}4 \\ -\ 86 \end{array}$$

Regroup tens.
$$\begin{array}{r} 9\\ 1\ \not{1}\not{0}\ 14\\ \not{2}\not{0}\not{4} \\ -\ 86 \end{array}$$

Subtract.
$$\begin{array}{r} 9\\ 1\ \not{1}\not{0}\ 14\\ \not{2}\not{0}\not{4} \\ -\ 86 \\ \hline 118 \end{array}$$

118 rocks were not painted.

B. Sometimes when you regroup, you will have 0 hundreds left.

Regroup hundreds.
$$\begin{array}{r} 0\ 10\\ \not{1}\not{0}0 \\ -\ 38 \end{array}$$

Regroup tens.
$$\begin{array}{r} 9\\ 0\ \not{1}\not{0}\ 10\\ \not{1}\not{0}\not{0} \\ -\ 38 \end{array}$$

Subtract.
$$\begin{array}{r} 9\\ 0\ \not{1}\not{0}\ 10\\ \not{1}\not{0}\not{0} \\ -\ 38 \\ \hline 62 \end{array}$$

TRY THESE

Subtract. Use addition to check.

1. 603 −157	**2.** 800 −743	**3.** 508 −146	**4.** 307 −109	**5.** $4.00 − .92	**6.** $7.00 − 3.65

7. 302 − 59 = ▦

8. 300 − 208 = ▦

9. $6.00 − $.97 = ▦

SKILLS PRACTICE

Subtract.

1. 605
   − 79

2. 504
   −268

3. 300
   − 7

4. 407
   − 84

5. 703
   −456

6. 806
   −382

7. 658
   −372

8. 203
   − 96

9. 300
   −206

10. 573
    −258

11. 607
    −219

12. 400
    − 8

13. 712
    −318

14. 903
    −297

15. 408
    −136

16. 406
    −287

17. $8.60
    − 3.50

18. $5.07
    − .59

19. 500 − 418 = ▨

20. 842 − 149 = ▨

21. 425 − 98 = ▨

22. 600 − 249 = ▨

23. 832 − 265 = ▨

24. $5.00 − $.47 = ▨

Add or subtract.

25. 302
    −174

26. 610
    +347

27. 804
    −781

28. 505
    −498

29. $2.05
    + 4.28

30. $7.08
    − 5.59

PROBLEM SOLVING

31. Mr. Cheng's class collected 308 rocks. They polished 119 of them. How many were left to polish?

32. Mrs. Wall had 500 arrowheads. She collected 60 more arrowheads. How many did she have then?

★33. Tina and her 3 brothers collected 125 rocks. Dan and his 2 brothers collected 99 rocks. How many people were collecting rocks?

★34. Alice paid $1.50 to go to the special rock exhibit at the museum. Her sister paid the same amount. How much did they spend in all?

EXTRA! Arranging Objects
This rock design is in the shape of a triangle. It points to the right. Make a triangle that points to the left by moving only 3 rocks.

SKILLS PRACTICE

Subtract. Use estimation to check.

1. $\begin{array}{r} 4,643 \\ -\ \ \ 999 \end{array}$	2. $\begin{array}{r} 6,654 \\ -1,742 \end{array}$	3. $\begin{array}{r} 754 \\ -\ \ 92 \end{array}$	4. $\begin{array}{r} 6,009 \\ -4,864 \end{array}$	5. $\begin{array}{r} 7,826 \\ -3,915 \end{array}$
6. $\begin{array}{r} 30,561 \\ -23,473 \end{array}$	7. $\begin{array}{r} 62,675 \\ -15,045 \end{array}$	8. $\begin{array}{r} 64,762 \\ -33,400 \end{array}$	9. $\begin{array}{r} 57,030 \\ -\ 2,455 \end{array}$	10. $\begin{array}{r} 28,644 \\ -\ 1,981 \end{array}$
11. $\begin{array}{r} 93,514 \\ -\ 9,606 \end{array}$	12. $\begin{array}{r} 48,015 \\ -\ 3,402 \end{array}$	13. $\begin{array}{r} 51,742 \\ -18,742 \end{array}$	14. $\begin{array}{r} \$551.73 \\ -\ \ 71.05 \end{array}$	15. $\begin{array}{r} \$695.01 \\ -\ 237.89 \end{array}$

16. $6,732 - 3,911 = $ ▨   17. $35,188 - 6,130 = $ ▨   18. $824 - 376 = $ ▨

19. $9,246 - 7,797 = $ ▨   20. $8,070 - 5,380 = $ ▨   ★21. $\$70.00 - \$.60 = $ ▨

Add or subtract. Use estimation to check.

22. $\begin{array}{r} 37,469 \\ -14,280 \end{array}$	23. $\begin{array}{r} 8,721 \\ +2,689 \end{array}$	24. $\begin{array}{r} 42,371 \\ +51,573 \end{array}$	25. $\begin{array}{r} \$143.82 \\ -\ \ 36.85 \end{array}$	26. $\begin{array}{r} \$243.82 \\ -\ \ 19.21 \end{array}$
27. $\begin{array}{r} 17,963 \\ -14,489 \end{array}$	28. $\begin{array}{r} 5,868 \\ -1,686 \end{array}$	29. $\begin{array}{r} 78,749 \\ +67,975 \end{array}$	30. $\begin{array}{r} 82,216 \\ +\ 4,739 \end{array}$	31. $\begin{array}{r} 96,742 \\ -10,008 \end{array}$

PROBLEM SOLVING

Solve. Use estimation to check.

32. The Music Center can hold 9,575 people. The City Center can hold 5,050 people. How many more people can the Music Center hold?

33. A businessman flew 5,256 km in July and 5,625 km in August. In what month did the businessman fly farther?

34. The Opera House seats 10,263 people. The Cosmopolitan Theater seats 15,632 people. How many more people can be seated in the Cosmopolitan Theater?

35. A runner ran a 41,374-meter marathon in September and a 34,052-meter marathon in October. How much farther did he run in October?

Workbook   page 406

Problem Solving: Estimates as Answers

Sometimes you don't need to know an exact answer. You may only need to know about how many. An estimate tells *about how many*.

A. 14,513 cars and 6,691 trucks traveled on the turnpike in one day. About how many more cars than trucks traveled on the turnpike?

$$
\begin{array}{r}
14,513 \longrightarrow 15,000 \\
-\ 6,691 \longrightarrow -\ 7,000 \\
\hline
8,000
\end{array}
$$

There were about 8,000 more cars than trucks.

B. A gas station made $22.59 selling oil on Friday and $31.19 selling oil on Saturday. About how much money did the station make selling oil?

$$
\begin{array}{r}
\$22.59 \longrightarrow \$20.00 \\
+\ 31.19 \longrightarrow +\ 30.00 \\
\hline
\$50.00
\end{array}
$$

The station made about $50.00.

TRY THESE

Solve each problem by estimating the sum or difference.

1. The Speedy Car Company produced 65,850 2-door cars and 41,490 4-door cars. About how many cars were produced in all?

2. Ms. Schwartz spent $36.89 for a new tire and $42.99 for a new battery. About how much did she spend for car parts?

PROBLEM SOLVING PRACTICE

Solve each problem by estimating the sum or difference.

1. 7,982 cars parked in one parking lot and 5,261 cars parked in another lot. About how many cars were in the two lots?

2. The Jensen family paid $9.69 for breakfast at a roadside restaurant. The Rossi family paid $8.25. About how much was paid in all?

3. 49,109 people traveled to the fair by bus. 71,800 traveled by train. About how many more people traveled by train than by bus?

4. 65,189 people went to the beach by car. The other 4,428 people went by bus. About how many people went to the beach in all?

5. There were 68,250 cars on the thruway. There were 9,572 buses. About how many fewer buses than cars were on the thruway?

6. In Auto City there are 6,479 sports cars and 4,920 station wagons. About how many sports cars and station wagons are there?

7. In Sun City, 5,500 people ride to work. 2,600 people walk to work. About how many people work in Sun City?

8. Mary is driving from Portland to Chicago. She has already driven 2,207 kilometers. She has 1,221 kilometers still to travel. About how far is Portland from Chicago?

★ 9. There are two bus routes on Highway 99. One driver collected $48.40. The other driver collected $51.80. About how much was collected in all?

★ 10. The tollbooth collector had $12.45 at noon. At 1 o'clock, he had $80.35. About how much money did he collect between noon and 1 o'clock?

Problem Solving: Finding Information

When you plan what to do, you must decide what numbers you will use. The numbers can be given in the problem, in a picture, or in a table.

1 Read the problem.
2 Plan what to do.
3 Do the arithmetic.
4 Give the answer.
5 Check your answer.

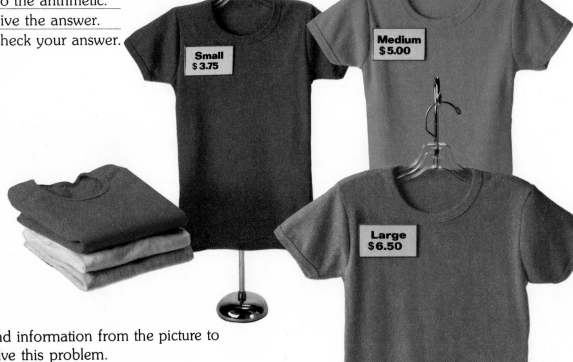

A. Find information from the picture to solve this problem.

Debbie bought a large T-shirt and a medium T-shirt. How much more did she spend for the large T-shirt?

$6.50
− 5.00
$1.50

Debbie spent $1.50 more for the large T-shirt.

B. Find information from the table to solve this problem.

Jan bought an extra large T-shirt for her father, a large T-shirt for her brother, and a small T-shirt for her sister. How much did she spend?

$7.25
6.50
+ 3.75
$17.50

Jan spent $17.50.

Size	Price
extra small	$3.50
small	$3.75
medium	$5.00
large	$6.50
extra large	$7.25

TRY THESE

Use the picture or the table to answer the questions.

BASKETBALL TICKET PRICE $10.95 EACH

FOOTBALL TICKET PRICE $12.50 EACH

Day	Number Sold	
	Basketball tickets	Football tickets
Monday	1,801	2,749
Tuesday	2,134	2,431
Wednesday	1,963	1,798
Thursday	1,488	2,003
Friday	2,259	2,891

1. How much does a basketball ticket cost?

2. How much does a football ticket cost?

3. How many football tickets were sold on Tuesday?

4. How many basketball tickets were sold on Friday?

PROBLEM SOLVING PRACTICE

Use the picture and table in Try These to solve these problems.

1. Laura bought a basketball ticket and a football ticket. How much money did she spend?

2. How much more does it cost to buy a football ticket than to buy a basketball ticket?

3. How many more basketball tickets were sold on Friday than on Monday?

4. How many more football tickets were sold on Tuesday than on Thursday?

5. Ann has $6.35. How much more does she need to buy a basketball ticket?

6. Eddie has $4.79. How much more does he need to buy a football ticket?

7. How many basketball tickets were sold in all during the week?

8. How many football tickets were sold in all during the week?

★ **9.** The manager said she would sell George three basketball tickets for $31.00. Is this a good buy?

★ **10.** The manager said she would sell Sally four football tickets for $52.00. Is this a good buy?

Unit Checkup

Add. *(pages 48–51)*

1. 43 +56	2. 39 +47	3. 86 +73	4. 99 +33	5. 78 +49

Add. *(pages 52–55)*

6. 234 +467	7. $5.89 + 6.96	8. 2,458 +9,867	9. 9,339 + 854	10. $22.39 + 1.43

11. $6 + 842 = $ ▨

12. $346 + 4,915 = $ ▨

13. $\$25.99 + \$78.88 = $ ▨

Find each sum. Then estimate to check your sum. *(pages 56–61)*

14. 7,549 +3,232	15. 5,555 +7,685	16. $ 83.94 + 676.59	17. 88,645 +69,427	18. 1,729 +46,788

Add. *(pages 62–63)*

19. 28 838 +928	20. 3,487 96,859 + 36	21. 35 183 25,609 + 3,824	22. 74,834 29 162 + 584	23. 25,879 6,076 389 +55,291

24. $381 + 7,994 + 18,212 = $ ▨

25. $618 + 49 + 13,207 = $ ▨

Subtract. *(pages 66–69)*

26. 98 −45	27. 87 −69	28. 489 −293	29. 665 − 83	30. $8.65 − 6.79

31. $545 - 489 = $ ▨

32. $653 - 29 = $ ▨

33. $\$8.24 - \$.95 = $ ▨

Find each difference. Then estimate to check your difference.
(pages 72–77)

34. $39.76 − 8.97	35. 49,664 −39,807	36. 6,329 −3,543	37. 92,776 −49,873	38. 83,291 − 7,622

Subtract. *(pages 70–71, 72–75)*

39. 800
− 38

40. 3,000
− 829

41. 60,001
−49,999

42. $130.00
− 96.48

43. 70,000
−58,406

44. 1,010 − 386 = ■

45. 50,006 − 4,962 = ■

Solve each problem. Then estimate to check your answer.
(pages 48–61, 66–79)

46. The Dover Library has 79,391 books. 12,385 are paperbacks. The rest are hardcover. How many books are hardcover?

47. 31,695 adults have library cards. 27,715 children have library cards. How many people have library cards?

48. There are 42,518 fiction books in the library. There are 9,847 biographies. How many more fiction books are there?

49. The library spent $246.32 on story books and $512.99 on reference books. How much money did it spend?

Use the picture and the table to solve the following problems. *(pages 80–81)*

Bookville Library Film Festival

Seasons	Number Sold	
	Books of Adults' Tickets	Book Childr
Summer	1,163	
Fall	909	
Winter	7?	
Spring		

50. Mr. Yamada bought a book of children's tickets and a book of adults' tickets. How much money did he spend?

51 Kim has $9.29. How much more money does she need to buy a book of children's tickets?

52. How many fewer books ~r? children's tickets wer~ the winter than in t'

83

Reinforcement

More Help with Addition

Add.

36	
+58	
94	

1. 23 +74

2. 18 +81

3. 25 +47

4. 29 +61

5. 44 +47

45
+65
110

6. 83 +83

7. 77 +51

8. 89 +43

9. 56 +65

10. 74 +98

612
+789
1,401

11. 342 +727

12. 853 +926

13. 248 +362

14. 767 +266

15. 823 +397

53,794
65

16. 1,379 +6,716

17. 8,397 +5,767

18. 89,867 +54,384

19. 93,674 +52,187

20. 7,164 +85,683

with Subtraction

btract.

952
−765
187

2. 93 −71

3. 34 −29

4. 86 −39

5. 75 −48

82,891
−35,684
47,207

11. 3,379 −1,839

8. 523 −449

9. 958 −369

10. 724 −393

70,000
− 931
69,069

16. 501 −266

17. 6,000 −3,639

85,352 7,569

14. 69,382 − 6,497

15. 38,683 − 6,791

18. 80, −34,78

70,009 26,374

20. 90,000 − 3,076

Expanded Form

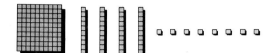

Standard Numeral   148

Expanded Form   100 + 40 + 8

A. To write the expanded form for a standard numeral, think of the meaning of its digits.

2,405

Meaning   2 thousands 4 hundreds 0 tens 5 ones

Expanded Form   2,000 + 400 + 5

You don't need to show the 0 tens.

Write the expanded form for each.

1. 1,586   **2.** 4,192   **3.** 85,734   **4.** 5,901   **5.** 20,075   **6.** 90

B. To write the standard numeral for a number shown in expanded form, use addition.

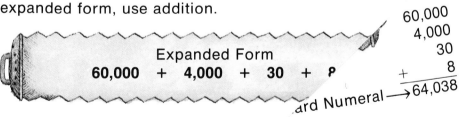

Expanded Form

60,000 + 4,000 + 30 + 8

60,000
4,000
30
+   8
_____
ard Numeral →64,038

Write the standard numeral for

7. 9,000 + 200 + 6

8. 6,000 + 700 + 50 + 2

9. 70,000 + 5,000 + 20

10. 800,000 + 50,000 + 200 + 6

11. 200,000 + 900 +

12. 50,000 + 7,000 + 6

Maintaining Skills

Choose the correct answer. Mark NG if the correct answer is NOT GIVEN.

1.   86
  +65
	2. 456
	  +323
		3. 6,578
		  + 424
			4. 82,962
			  + 7,054

a. 141 **b.** 151 **c.** 21 **d.** NG	**a.** 133 **b.** 797 **c.** 779 **d.** NG	**a.** 7,002 **b.** 6,154 **c.** 6,992 **d.** NG	**a.** 89,916 **b.** 85,912 **c.** 90,016 **d.** NG

5.   4
    4
  +4
	6. 16
	    28
	  +49
		7. 482
		    95
		  +184
			8. 6,382
			    149
			  +2,476

a. 8 **b.** 21	**a.** 93 **b.** 83 **c.** 73 **d.** NG	**a.** 661 **b.** 651 **c.** 751 **d.** NG	**a.** 8,997 **b.** 9,007 **c.** 8,907 **d.** NG

a. 13
b. 21
c. 182
d. NG
	10. 705
	  −684
	
	    12
		11. 5,000
		  −4,691
		
		a. 319
		b. 419
		c. 309
		d. NG
			12. $605.00
			  − 92.00
			
			a. $531.00
			b. $613.00
			c. $513.00
			d. NG

13. 80,900 people visited the park in July. 79,080 people visited it in August. How many more people visited the state park in July?

  a. 1,810 people
  b. 11,020 people
  c. 1,920 people
  d. NG

14. A forest ranger drove her jeep 708 kilometers during May. She drove 1,003 kilometers during June. How many kilometers did she drive in all?

  a. 1,711 kilometers
  b. 1,705 kilometers
  c. 1,711 kilometers
  d. NG

Multiplication and Division 4

Multiplying by 2 or 3

A. Sally has 2 boxes of plants.
There are 6 plants in each box.
How many plants are there in all?

You can **multiply** to find how many in all, when
the sets have the same number in each.

$$2 \times 6 = 12 \qquad \begin{array}{r} 6 \\ \times\ 2 \\ \hline 12 \end{array}$$

B. The numbers you multiply are called the **factors.**
The answer is called the **product.**

$$3 \times 7 = 21 \qquad \begin{array}{r} 7 \\ \times 3 \\ \hline 21 \end{array}$$

factors   product   factors   product

A product is a **multiple** of each of its factors.

C. $3 \times 7 = 21$ A fact written in this form is a **number sentence.**

TRY THESE

Multiply to find the products. Look for patterns.

1.

$\begin{array}{r}1\\\times2\\\hline\end{array}$	$\begin{array}{r}2\\\times2\\\hline\end{array}$	$\begin{array}{r}3\\\times2\\\hline\end{array}$	$\begin{array}{r}4\\\times2\\\hline\end{array}$	$\begin{array}{r}5\\\times2\\\hline\end{array}$	$\begin{array}{r}6\\\times2\\\hline\end{array}$	$\begin{array}{r}7\\\times2\\\hline\end{array}$	$\begin{array}{r}8\\\times2\\\hline\end{array}$	$\begin{array}{r}9\\\times2\\\hline\end{array}$

2.

$\begin{array}{r}1\\\times3\\\hline\end{array}$	$\begin{array}{r}2\\\times3\\\hline\end{array}$	$\begin{array}{r}3\\\times3\\\hline\end{array}$	$\begin{array}{r}4\\\times3\\\hline\end{array}$	$\begin{array}{r}5\\\times3\\\hline\end{array}$	$\begin{array}{r}6\\\times3\\\hline\end{array}$	$\begin{array}{r}7\\\times3\\\hline\end{array}$	$\begin{array}{r}8\\\times3\\\hline\end{array}$	$\begin{array}{r}9\\\times3\\\hline\end{array}$

Complete the number sentences.

3. $2 \times 4 = $ ▧

4. $3 \times 5 = $ ▧

5. $3 \times 9 = $ ▧

SKILLS PRACTICE

Multiply.

1. 3
    ×2

2. 1
    ×3

3. 6
    ×2

4. 5
    ×3

5. 2
    ×2

6. 4
    ×2

7. 7
    ×3

8. 6
    ×3

9. 8
    ×2

10. 1
    ×2

11. 4
    ×3

12. 7
    ×2

13. 9
    ×2

14. 2
    ×3

15. $3 \times 9 =$ ▧

16. $2 \times 5 =$ ▧

17. $3 \times 8 =$ ▧

18. $3 \times 6 =$ ▧

19. $2 \times 7 =$ ▧

20. $3 \times 5 =$ ▧

Look at this fact.

$$3 \times 9 = 27$$

21. What are the factors?

22. What is the product?

23. Find the product of 2 and 6.

24. Multiply 3 times 8.

25. One factor is 2. The other factor is 7. What is the product?

★ 26. One factor is 3. The product is 24. What is the other factor?

PROBLEM SOLVING

27. Joel has 3 baskets of tomatoes. He has 8 tomatoes in each. How many tomatoes does he have?

28. Anna has 2 boxes of squash. There are 7 squash in each. How many squash does she have?

Multiplying by 4 or 5

Steve saw 5 bicycles.
There were 2 wheels on each bicycle.
How many wheels did he see?

5 sets of 2 wheels
$$5 \times 2 = 10$$

You could add
$2+2+2+2+2 = 10$.
But it's easier
to multiply.

Steve saw 10 wheels.

TRY THESE

Multiply to find the products. Look for patterns.

1.	1 ×4	2 ×4	3 ×4	4 ×4	5 ×4	6 ×4	7 ×4	8 ×4	9 ×4

2.	1 ×5	2 ×5	3 ×5	4 ×5	5 ×5	6 ×5	7 ×5	8 ×5	9 ×5

Multiply.

3. 8 ×5	4. 9 ×4	5. 6 ×4	6. 5 ×5	7. 7 ×4	8. 8 ×4	9. 4 ×4

10. $5 \times 6 =$ ■   **11.** $4 \times 6 =$ ■   **12.** $5 \times 5 =$ ■

SKILLS PRACTICE

Multiply.

1. $\begin{array}{r} 6 \\ \times 2 \\ \hline \end{array}$
2. $\begin{array}{r} 5 \\ \times 4 \\ \hline \end{array}$
3. $\begin{array}{r} 3 \\ \times 3 \\ \hline \end{array}$
4. $\begin{array}{r} 2 \\ \times 4 \\ \hline \end{array}$
5. $\begin{array}{r} 3 \\ \times 2 \\ \hline \end{array}$
6. $\begin{array}{r} 5 \\ \times 2 \\ \hline \end{array}$
7. $\begin{array}{r} 4 \\ \times 4 \\ \hline \end{array}$

8. $\begin{array}{r} 6 \\ \times 3 \\ \hline \end{array}$
9. $\begin{array}{r} 4 \\ \times 2 \\ \hline \end{array}$
10. $\begin{array}{r} 5 \\ \times 5 \\ \hline \end{array}$
11. $\begin{array}{r} 3 \\ \times 4 \\ \hline \end{array}$
12. $\begin{array}{r} 4 \\ \times 5 \\ \hline \end{array}$
13. $\begin{array}{r} 5 \\ \times 3 \\ \hline \end{array}$
14. $\begin{array}{r} 2 \\ \times 5 \\ \hline \end{array}$

15. $\begin{array}{r} 9 \\ \times 4 \\ \hline \end{array}$
16. $\begin{array}{r} 7 \\ \times 3 \\ \hline \end{array}$
17. $\begin{array}{r} 8 \\ \times 2 \\ \hline \end{array}$
18. $\begin{array}{r} 9 \\ \times 5 \\ \hline \end{array}$
19. $\begin{array}{r} 3 \\ \times 5 \\ \hline \end{array}$
20. $\begin{array}{r} 7 \\ \times 4 \\ \hline \end{array}$
21. $\begin{array}{r} 9 \\ \times 3 \\ \hline \end{array}$

22. $\begin{array}{r} 7 \\ \times 2 \\ \hline \end{array}$
23. $\begin{array}{r} 6 \\ \times 5 \\ \hline \end{array}$
24. $\begin{array}{r} 6 \\ \times 4 \\ \hline \end{array}$
25. $\begin{array}{r} 7 \\ \times 5 \\ \hline \end{array}$
26. $\begin{array}{r} 2 \\ \times 2 \\ \hline \end{array}$
27. $\begin{array}{r} 8 \\ \times 3 \\ \hline \end{array}$
28. $\begin{array}{r} 2 \\ \times 3 \\ \hline \end{array}$

29. $5 \times 8 = $ ▨
30. $4 \times 8 = $ ▨
31. $2 \times 9 = $ ▨

32. $4 \times 7 = $ ▨
33. $3 \times 8 = $ ▨
34. $5 \times 9 = $ ▨

35. Multiply 5 times 7.

36. Find the product of 4 and 9.

★ 37. One factor is 5. The product is 45. What is the other factor?

PROBLEM SOLVING

38. 4 girls wanted to put streamers on their bikes. Each girl used 5 meters of streamer paper. How much paper did they use in all?

39. George had 5 bike locks. Marcia had 4 locks. How many more locks did George have?

40. There were 5 bike racks. Each rack held 7 bikes. How many bikes did the racks hold?

41. 5 riders sat down to rest. 7 more riders joined them. How many riders were resting?

Multiplying by 6 or 7

Karen bought 6 records.
There were 5 songs on each record.
How many songs did she buy in all?

   6 sets of 5
   6 × 5 = 30

There were 30 songs in all.

TRY THESE

Multiply to find the products. Look for patterns.

1.

1	2	3	4	5	6	7	8	9
×6	×6	×6	×6	×6	×6	×6	×6	×6

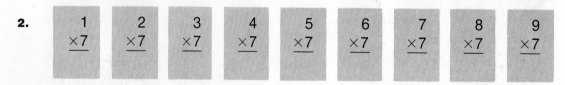

2.

1	2	3	4	5	6	7	8	9
×7	×7	×7	×7	×7	×7	×7	×7	×7

Complete the number sentences.

3. 7 × 5 = ▧   4. 6 × 3 = ▧   5. 6 × 9 = ▧

6. 7 × 7 = ▧   7. 7 × 4 = ▧   8. 6 × 7 = ▧

SKILLS PRACTICE

Multiply.

1. 3
×7

2. 4
×3

3. 8
×6

4. 3
×6

5. 4
×4

6. 2
×7

7. 2
×5

8. 4
×5

9. 7
×6

10. 2
×6

11. 7
×3

12. 6
×5

13. 8
×4

14. 8
×2

15. 7
×7

16. 4
×6

17. 6
×3

18. 2
×2

19. 4
×7

20. 5
×5

21. 9
×4

22. 6
×6

23. 6
×7

24. 3
×4

25. 8
×5

26. 5
×7

27. 3
×5

28. 9
×3

29. 5
×6

30. 8
×5

31. 8
×7

32. 5
×4

33. 8
×3

34. 5
×3

35. 9
×7

36. $3 \times 5 = $ ▨

37. $6 \times 9 = $ ▨

38. $3 \times 3 = $ ▨

39. $5 \times 9 = $ ▨

40. $4 \times 2 = $ ▨

41. $5 \times 7 = $ ▨

PROBLEM SOLVING

42. Karen bought 6 records last week and 7 records this week. How many records did she buy in all?

43. Bob played 6 records. There were 7 songs on each. How many songs did he play?

44. Sue bought 7 albums. Each album contained 2 records. How many records did she buy?

45. Angie had 7 records. Justin had 2 records. How many records did they have in all?

★46. Juan had 2 45-rpm records and 3 33⅓-rpm records. How many records did he have in all?

★47. A 45-rpm record has 4 songs on it. A 33⅓-rpm record has 7 songs on it. Which record has more songs on it?

Multiplying by 8 or 9

The roller coaster has 9 cars with 6 people in each.
How many people are riding on the roller coaster?

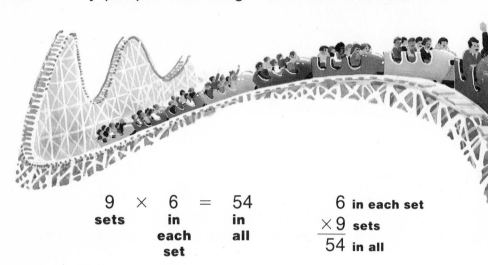

$$9 \times 6 = 54$$

sets   in   in
       each all
       set

$$\begin{array}{r} 6 \text{ in each set} \\ \times 9 \text{ sets} \\ \hline 54 \text{ in all} \end{array}$$

54 people are riding on the roller coaster.

TRY THESE

Multiply to find the products. Look for patterns.

1.

$\begin{array}{r}1\\\times 8\end{array}$	$\begin{array}{r}2\\\times 8\end{array}$	$\begin{array}{r}3\\\times 8\end{array}$	$\begin{array}{r}4\\\times 8\end{array}$	$\begin{array}{r}5\\\times 8\end{array}$	$\begin{array}{r}6\\\times 8\end{array}$	$\begin{array}{r}7\\\times 8\end{array}$	$\begin{array}{r}8\\\times 8\end{array}$	$\begin{array}{r}9\\\times 8\end{array}$

2.

$\begin{array}{r}1\\\times 9\end{array}$	$\begin{array}{r}2\\\times 9\end{array}$	$\begin{array}{r}3\\\times 9\end{array}$	$\begin{array}{r}4\\\times 9\end{array}$	$\begin{array}{r}5\\\times 9\end{array}$	$\begin{array}{r}6\\\times 9\end{array}$	$\begin{array}{r}7\\\times 9\end{array}$	$\begin{array}{r}8\\\times 9\end{array}$	$\begin{array}{r}9\\\times 9\end{array}$

Complete the number sentences.

3. $8 \times 2 = $ ▧

4. $9 \times 8 = $ ▧

5. $8 \times 9 = $ ▧

6. $8 \times 4 = $ ▧

7. $9 \times 9 = $ ▧

8. $9 \times 7 = $ ▧

SKILLS PRACTICE

Multiply.

1. $\begin{array}{r}4\\ \times 8\\ \hline\end{array}$	**2.** $\begin{array}{r}6\\ \times 7\\ \hline\end{array}$	**3.** $\begin{array}{r}3\\ \times 5\\ \hline\end{array}$	**4.** $\begin{array}{r}9\\ \times 5\\ \hline\end{array}$	**5.** $\begin{array}{r}2\\ \times 9\\ \hline\end{array}$	**6.** $\begin{array}{r}3\\ \times 8\\ \hline\end{array}$	**7.** $\begin{array}{r}7\\ \times 9\\ \hline\end{array}$
8. $\begin{array}{r}5\\ \times 6\\ \hline\end{array}$	**9.** $\begin{array}{r}8\\ \times 7\\ \hline\end{array}$	**10.** $\begin{array}{r}4\\ \times 6\\ \hline\end{array}$	**11.** $\begin{array}{r}5\\ \times 9\\ \hline\end{array}$	**12.** $\begin{array}{r}4\\ \times 4\\ \hline\end{array}$	**13.** $\begin{array}{r}3\\ \times 7\\ \hline\end{array}$	**14.** $\begin{array}{r}8\\ \times 8\\ \hline\end{array}$
15. $\begin{array}{r}6\\ \times 8\\ \hline\end{array}$	**16.** $\begin{array}{r}2\\ \times 6\\ \hline\end{array}$	**17.** $\begin{array}{r}9\\ \times 3\\ \hline\end{array}$	**18.** $\begin{array}{r}7\\ \times 8\\ \hline\end{array}$	**19.** $\begin{array}{r}7\\ \times 5\\ \hline\end{array}$	**20.** $\begin{array}{r}3\\ \times 4\\ \hline\end{array}$	**21.** $\begin{array}{r}4\\ \times 9\\ \hline\end{array}$
22. $\begin{array}{r}9\\ \times 6\\ \hline\end{array}$	**23.** $\begin{array}{r}9\\ \times 2\\ \hline\end{array}$	**24.** $\begin{array}{r}6\\ \times 8\\ \hline\end{array}$	**25.** $\begin{array}{r}9\\ \times 8\\ \hline\end{array}$	**26.** $\begin{array}{r}3\\ \times 6\\ \hline\end{array}$	**27.** $\begin{array}{r}9\\ \times 9\\ \hline\end{array}$	**28.** $\begin{array}{r}2\\ \times 8\\ \hline\end{array}$

29. $7 \times 7 = $ **30.** $3 \times 9 = $ **31.** $7 \times 9 = $

32. $9 \times 6 = $ **33.** $8 \times 5 = $ **34.** $9 \times 8 = $

35. Find the product of 8 and 9.   **36.** Multiply 9 times 5.

★ **37.** One factor is 8. The product is 40. What is the other factor?

PROBLEM SOLVING

38. There are 8 cars on the space shuttle ride. Each car holds 4 people. How many people can ride the space shuttle?

39. 8 adults and 4 children all bought space shuttle tickets. How many tickets were bought?

40. There are 9 super boats. Each holds 6 people. How many people can ride on the super boats?

41. Tammy bought 8 books of tickets. Each book contains 9 tickets. How many tickets did she buy?

Multiplication Properties

These pictures show a property of multiplication.

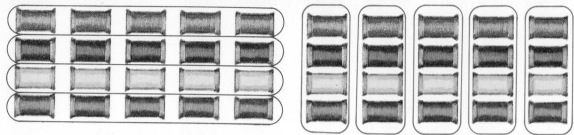

4 sets of 5 = 20
4 × 5 = 20

5 sets of 4 = 20
5 × 4 = 20

4 × 5 = 5 × 4

$$\begin{array}{cc} 4 & 5 \\ \times 5 & \times 4 \\ \hline 20 & 20 \end{array}$$

When you change the order of the factors, the product does not change.

ORDER PROPERTY

Zero and one have special properties as factors.

$$\begin{array}{cc} 3 & 0 \\ \times 0 & \times 4 \\ \hline 0 & 0 \end{array}$$

When you use 0 as a factor, the product is 0.

PROPERTY OF ZERO

$$\begin{array}{cc} 3 & 1 \\ \times 1 & \times 4 \\ \hline 3 & 4 \end{array}$$

When you use 1 as a factor, the product is the same as the other factor.

PROPERTY OF ONE

TRY THESE

Complete the number sentences.

1. 7 × 5 = ▨
   5 × 7 = ▨

2. 8 × 4 = ▨
   4 × 8 = ▨

3. 8 × 5 = ▨
   5 × 8 = ▨

Multiply.

4. $\begin{array}{r} 4 \\ \times 0 \\ \hline \end{array}$

5. $\begin{array}{r} 0 \\ \times 6 \\ \hline \end{array}$

6. $\begin{array}{r} 0 \\ \times 0 \\ \hline \end{array}$

7. $\begin{array}{r} 1 \\ \times 0 \\ \hline \end{array}$

8. $\begin{array}{r} 1 \\ \times 3 \\ \hline \end{array}$

9. $\begin{array}{r} 6 \\ \times 1 \\ \hline \end{array}$

10. $\begin{array}{r} 1 \\ \times 1 \\ \hline \end{array}$

SKILLS PRACTICE

Multiply.

1. $\begin{array}{r} 0 \\ \times 5 \\ \hline \end{array}$
2. $\begin{array}{r} 6 \\ \times 3 \\ \hline \end{array}$
3. $\begin{array}{r} 4 \\ \times 1 \\ \hline \end{array}$
4. $\begin{array}{r} 8 \\ \times 6 \\ \hline \end{array}$
5. $\begin{array}{r} 9 \\ \times 4 \\ \hline \end{array}$
6. $\begin{array}{r} 4 \\ \times 6 \\ \hline \end{array}$
7. $\begin{array}{r} 7 \\ \times 6 \\ \hline \end{array}$

8. $\begin{array}{r} 8 \\ \times 3 \\ \hline \end{array}$
9. $\begin{array}{r} 7 \\ \times 1 \\ \hline \end{array}$
10. $\begin{array}{r} 2 \\ \times 9 \\ \hline \end{array}$
11. $\begin{array}{r} 4 \\ \times 8 \\ \hline \end{array}$
12. $\begin{array}{r} 7 \\ \times 7 \\ \hline \end{array}$
13. $\begin{array}{r} 5 \\ \times 7 \\ \hline \end{array}$
14. $\begin{array}{r} 4 \\ \times 5 \\ \hline \end{array}$

15. $\begin{array}{r} 2 \\ \times 5 \\ \hline \end{array}$
16. $\begin{array}{r} 8 \\ \times 0 \\ \hline \end{array}$
17. $\begin{array}{r} 6 \\ \times 6 \\ \hline \end{array}$
18. $\begin{array}{r} 7 \\ \times 9 \\ \hline \end{array}$
19. $\begin{array}{r} 1 \\ \times 6 \\ \hline \end{array}$
20. $\begin{array}{r} 8 \\ \times 7 \\ \hline \end{array}$
21. $\begin{array}{r} 5 \\ \times 8 \\ \hline \end{array}$

22. $\begin{array}{r} 9 \\ \times 6 \\ \hline \end{array}$
23. $\begin{array}{r} 5 \\ \times 9 \\ \hline \end{array}$
24. $\begin{array}{r} 9 \\ \times 8 \\ \hline \end{array}$
25. $\begin{array}{r} 6 \\ \times 0 \\ \hline \end{array}$
26. $\begin{array}{r} 5 \\ \times 5 \\ \hline \end{array}$
27. $\begin{array}{r} 7 \\ \times 4 \\ \hline \end{array}$
28. $\begin{array}{r} 9 \\ \times 9 \\ \hline \end{array}$

29. $9 \times 3 = $ ▩
30. $8 \times 8 = $ ▩
31. $3 \times 0 = $ ▩

32. $8 \times 1 = $ ▩
★ 33. $0 \times 276 = $ ▩
★ 34. $1 \times 485 = $ ▩

35. Use the numbers 4 and 6 as factors. Write two multiplication facts.

36. One factor is 0. The other factor is 8. What is the product?

37. One factor is 1. The other factor is 9. What is the product?

★ 38. What is the product of 379 and 0?

★ 39. What is the product of 832 and 1?

★ 40. Since $4 \times 32 = 128$, what does 32×4 equal?

PROBLEM SOLVING

The Sewing Shop keeps a record of the kinds of buttons it has in stock. Copy and complete the records.

	Kind of Button	Cards	Buttons on each	In all
41.	Wood	4	7	▩
42.	Plastic	6	8	▩
43.	Leather	3	1	▩

	Kind of Button	Cards	Buttons on each	In all
44.	Metal	5	3	▩
45.	Cloth	2	8	▩
46.	Bone	1	6	▩

Problem Solving: Multiplying with Money

You can use multiplication to solve problems using money.

1 | **Read the problem.**

There are 4 games on the shelf.
Each game costs $5.
How much do the games cost in all?

> How much do
> 4 games cost?

2 | **Plan what to do.**

What operation should you use?

What numbers should you use?

4 sets of 5. Multiply.

3 | **Do the arithmetic.**

$$\begin{array}{r} 5 \\ \times\,4 \\ \hline 20 \end{array}$$

4 | **Give the answer.**   The games cost $20.

5 | **Check your answer.**

Use the Order Property.

$$\begin{array}{r} 4 \\ \times\,5 \\ \hline 20\checkmark \end{array}$$

TRY THESE

Choose the operation. Draw a picture if needed.

1. Laura bought 8 stamp albums. Each stamp album cost $5. How much did she spend?

2. Ben gave Laura 8 envelopes with 5 stamps on each. How many stamps did he give her?

3. Each page of the album has room for 8 stamps. Laura has pasted 5 stamps on a page. How many more can she paste on that page?

4. A stamp album costs $5. A photo album costs $8. Sandy bought one of each. How much did she spend?

PROBLEM SOLVING PRACTICE _____

Use the five steps to solve each problem. Draw a picture if needed.

1. Peter bought 3 foreign coins. Each coin cost $8. How much did he spend?

2. 5 students collect stamps. 9 students collect coins. How many more students collect coins?

3. Jon bought 3 sets of animal stamps. 7 stamps are in each set. How many stamps did he buy?

4. A zebra stamp costs $6. An elephant stamp costs $2. Which stamp costs more?

5. A kit of wildlife stamps costs $2. A kit of space stamps costs $5. How much will it cost to buy both?

6. A package of French stamps costs $7. Al bought 4 packages. How much did he spend?

7. Mrs. Conrad sold seven coins. Each was worth nine dollars. How much did she collect?

8. An old U.S. stamp was worth $3. Joseph bought 4 of them. How much did he spend?

★ 9. Seven new stamps were printed in one year. Eight new stamps were printed in the next year. How many new stamps were printed in these two years?

★ 10. Mr. Reilly bought 3 valuable stamps for $6 each. How much did the stamps cost? Did he receive any change from a twenty dollar bill? How much change?

Make up a money problem for each number sentence.

★ 11. $4 \times 7 = $ ▨

★ 12. $6 \times 3 = $ ▨

Missing Factors

Mike's homework paper ripped on his way home from school. To rewrite his multiplication facts, he must find the *missing factors.*

For the first fact, he must think of what number times 2 is 8.

$\blacksquare \times 2 = 8$

$1 \times 2 = 2$ Too small.
$2 \times 2 = 4$ Too small.
$3 \times 2 = 6$ Too small.
$4 \times 2 = 8$ Just right!

4 is the missing factor. $4 \times 2 = 8$

To complete the second and third facts he thinks:

$2 \times 4 = 8$
$3 \times 4 = 12$
$4 \times 4 = 16$
$5 \times 4 = 20$

$3 \times 2 = 6$
$3 \times 3 = 9$
$3 \times 4 = 12$

$\blacksquare \times 4 = 20$ $3 \times \blacksquare = 12$

5 is the missing factor.   4 is the missing factor.

TRY THESE

Find the missing factors.

1. $\blacksquare \times 2 = 4$
2. $\blacksquare \times 2 = 6$
3. $\blacksquare \times 2 = 16$
4. $\blacksquare \times 2 = 18$

5. $\blacksquare \times 3 = 9$
6. $\blacksquare \times 3 = 15$
7. $\blacksquare \times 3 = 21$
8. $\blacksquare \times 3 = 27$

9. $\blacksquare \times 5 = 10$
10. $\blacksquare \times 5 = 25$
11. $\blacksquare \times 5 = 35$
12. $\blacksquare \times 5 = 45$

SKILLS PRACTICE

Find the missing factors.

1. ▦ × 2 = 4   2. ▦ × 2 = 12   3. ▦ × 2 = 18

4. ▦ × 3 = 15   5. ▦ × 3 = 9   6. ▦ × 3 = 24

7. ▦ × 4 = 20   8. ▦ × 4 = 32   9. ▦ × 4 = 36

10. ▦ × 5 = 25   11. ▦ × 5 = 35   12. ▦ × 5 = 45

13. ▦ × 3 = 12   14. ▦ × 5 = 15   15. ▦ × 4 = 16

16. 3 × ▦ = 12   17. 5 × ▦ = 15   18. 4 × ▦ = 16

19. 5   20. 6   21. 8   22. 3   23. 4   24. 2
   × ▦   × ▦   × ▦   × ▦   × ▦   × ▦
   ‾‾‾‾   ‾‾‾‾   ‾‾‾‾   ‾‾‾   ‾‾‾   ‾‾‾‾
     10   18   40   9   8   10

25. 9   26. 8   27. ▦   28. 6   29. 9   30. ▦
   × ▦   × ▦   × 5   × ▦   × ▦   × 5
   ‾‾‾‾   ‾‾‾‾   ‾‾‾‾   ‾‾‾‾   ‾‾‾‾   ‾‾‾‾
     45   32   25   30   36   20

PROBLEM SOLVING

31. Ms. Antico had $35. She had only $5 bills. How many bills did she have?

32. Mr. Diaz had $8. He had only $1 bills. How many bills did he have?

★ 33. Copy and complete the tables.

roller skates	1	2		4					
wheels	4		12		20	24	28	32	36

★ 34.

pairs of roller skates	1	2		4					
wheels	8		24		40	48	56	64	72

a Maintaining Skills

Round to the nearest ten.

1. 68   **2.** 47   **3.** 24   **4.** 85   **5.** 93

Round to the nearest hundred.

6. 432   **7.** 689   **8.** 146   **9.** 755   **10.** 698

Round to the nearest thousand.

11. 5,283   **12.** 8,975   **13.** 21,563   **14.** 37,487   **15.** 9,987

Add.

16.	**17.**	**18.**	**19.**	**20.**
2,723	3,637	$45,684	$73,629	$68,457
+ 629	+7,363	+ 7,905	+ 59,793	+ 31,543

Subtract.

21.	**22.**	**23.**	**24.**	**25.**
7,523	4,895	$25,841	$68,425	$43,591
−1,495	− 799	− 16,953	− 4,917	− 9,788

Add or subtract.

26.	**27.**	**28.**	**29.**	**30.**
60	896	7,531	1,634	99,002
−19	+371	−4,163	+ 266	−98,471

31. 56 − 18 = ▤   **32.** 39 + 45 = ▤   **33.** 253 + 869 = ▤

34. 1,734 + 3,927 = ▤   **35.** 5,037 − 739 = ▤   **36.** 24,632 − 16,847 = ▤

Solve the problems.

37. 7,426 people voted for Ms. Gannon. 6,985 people voted for Mr. Arnold. How many more people voted for Ms. Gannon?

38. 8,627 people voted at one school and 8,792 people voted at another school. How many people voted in all?

39. 19,104 people were registered to vote at the two schools. 17,637 people actually voted. How many people did not vote?

40. Out of the 17,637 votes, 289 could not be used. How many votes could be used?

Project: Even-Odd Systems

When the gasoline supply is limited, some states use an even-odd system. People with *even-numbered* license plates can buy gas only on *even-numbered* days of the month. People with *odd-numbered* license plates can buy gas only on *odd-numbered* days.

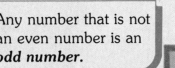

Any number that is a multiple of 2 is an **even number.**

Any number that is not an even number is an **odd number.**

Even Numbers

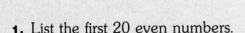

Odd Numbers

1. List the first 20 even numbers.

2. The digit in the ones place of an even number is always ■, ■, ■, ■, or ■.

3. List the first 20 odd numbers.

4. The digit in the ones place of an odd number is always ■, ■, ■, ■, or ■.

Is the number even or odd?

5. 44   6. 169   7. 200   8. 1,466   9. 7,853

10. List the license plates shown at the right whose owners can buy gas on September 30.

11. List the license plates shown at the right whose owners can buy gas on August 19.

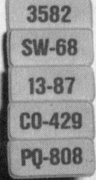

Has your state ever used a system to tell when people could buy gas? If it has, what was the system?

Make up a fair system for using license plates to buy gas with letter combinations like these.

Dividing by 2 or 3

A. You can *divide* to find the number of sets when you know the number in all and the number in each set.

Number
in each box
↓

$$12 \div 2 = \blacksquare$$

↑ Number
in all

↑ Number
of boxes

so

boxes   in each
↓   box
↓

$$6 \times 2 = 12 \leftarrow \text{in all}$$

$$12 \div 2 = 6 \leftarrow \text{boxes}$$

↑ in all   ↑ in each
box

B. 6 in all
2 in each set
How many sets?

$$6 \div 2 = \blacksquare \quad \text{or} \quad 2\overline{)6}$$

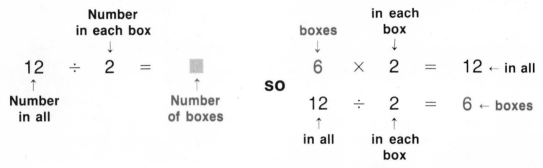

To find the number of sets, think of a **missing factor.**

$\blacksquare \times 2 = 6$
$1 \times 2 = 2$ Too small.
$2 \times 2 = 4$ Too small.
$3 \times 2 = 6$ **Just right!**

$$3 \times 2 = 6 \quad \text{so} \quad 6 \div 2 = 3 \quad \text{or} \quad 2\overset{3}{\overline{)6}}$$

TRY THESE

Divide.

1. $2\overline{)2}$ $\blacksquare \times 2 = 2$
2. $2\overline{)4}$ $\blacksquare \times 2 = 4$
3. $2\overline{)6}$ $\blacksquare \times 2 = 6$
4. $2\overline{)8}$ $\blacksquare \times 2 = 8$
5. $2\overline{)10}$ $\blacksquare \times 2 = 10$
6. $2\overline{)12}$ $\blacksquare \times 2 = 12$
7. $2\overline{)14}$ $\blacksquare \times 2 = 14$
8. $2\overline{)16}$ $\blacksquare \times 2 = 16$
9. $2\overline{)18}$ $\blacksquare \times 2 = 18$

10. $3\overline{)3}$ $\blacksquare \times 3 = 3$
11. $3\overline{)6}$ $\blacksquare \times 3 = 6$
12. $3\overline{)9}$ $\blacksquare \times 3 = 9$
13. $3\overline{)12}$ $\blacksquare \times 3 = 12$
14. $3\overline{)15}$ $\blacksquare \times 3 = 15$
15. $3\overline{)18}$ $\blacksquare \times 3 = 18$
16. $3\overline{)21}$ $\blacksquare \times 3 = 21$
17. $3\overline{)24}$ $\blacksquare \times 3 = 24$
18. $3\overline{)27}$ $\blacksquare \times 3 = 27$

SKILLS PRACTICE

Divide.

1. $3\overline{)15}$ 2. $2\overline{)14}$ 3. $2\overline{)8}$ 4. $3\overline{)9}$ 5. $3\overline{)24}$ 6. $2\overline{)6}$

7. $2\overline{)16}$ 8. $2\overline{)12}$ 9. $3\overline{)12}$ 10. $3\overline{)27}$ 11. $3\overline{)18}$ 12. $2\overline{)18}$

13. $2\overline{)4}$ 14. $2\overline{)10}$ 15. $3\overline{)3}$ 16. $3\overline{)6}$ 17. $3\overline{)21}$ 18. $2\overline{)2}$

19. $16 \div 2 = \blacksquare$ 20. $24 \div 3 = \blacksquare$ 21. $10 \div 2 = \blacksquare$

22. $21 \div 3 = \blacksquare$ 23. $27 \div 3 = \blacksquare$ 24. $18 \div 2 = \blacksquare$

Look at this division.

$$\text{apples} \rightarrow 2\overline{)14} \overset{\text{7 baskets}}{\text{ apples}}$$
in each basket

★ 25. Which number tells how many in all?

★ 26. Which number tells how many in each set?

★ 27. Which number tells how many sets?

Upside-down answers 8 .61

Dividing by 4 or 5

A. Cathy has 12 baseballs.
There are 4 baseballs in each box.
How many boxes does she have?

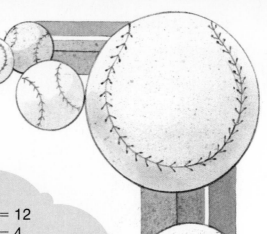

In each
box $\longrightarrow$ $4\overline{)12}$ $\longleftarrow$ In all

$\blacksquare \times 4 = 12$
$1 \times 4 = 4$
$2 \times 4 = 8$
$3 \times 4 = 12$ **Just right!**

$3 \times 4 = 12$ so $4\overline{)12}^{3}$ Cathy has 3 boxes.

B. Numbers in division have special names.

$4\overline{)12}$ with $3 \longleftarrow$ **Quotient**, Divisor $\longleftarrow 4\overline{)12} \longleftarrow$ **Dividend**

Dividend **Divisor**
↓   ↓
$12 \div 4 = 3 \leftarrow$ **Quotient**

TRY THESE

1. $4\overline{)4}$ $\blacksquare \times 4 = 4$
2. $4\overline{)8}$ $\blacksquare \times 4 = 8$
3. $4\overline{)12}$ $\blacksquare \times 4 = 12$
4. $4\overline{)16}$ $\blacksquare \times 4 = 16$
5. $4\overline{)20}$ $\blacksquare \times 4 = 20$
6. $4\overline{)24}$ $\blacksquare \times 4 = 24$
7. $4\overline{)28}$ $\blacksquare \times 4 = 28$
8. $4\overline{)32}$ $\blacksquare \times 4 = 32$
9. $4\overline{)36}$ $\blacksquare \times 4 = 36$

10. $5\overline{)5}$ $\blacksquare \times 5 = 5$
11. $5\overline{)10}$ $\blacksquare \times 5 = 10$
12. $5\overline{)15}$ $\blacksquare \times 5 = 15$
13. $5\overline{)20}$ $\blacksquare \times 5 = 20$
14. $5\overline{)25}$ $\blacksquare \times 5 = 25$
15. $5\overline{)30}$ $\blacksquare \times 5 = 30$
16. $5\overline{)35}$ $\blacksquare \times 5 = 35$
17. $5\overline{)40}$ $\blacksquare \times 5 = 40$
18. $5\overline{)45}$ $\blacksquare \times 5 = 45$

SKILLS PRACTICE

Divide.

1. $5\overline{)35}$ 2. $4\overline{)20}$ 3. $4\overline{)12}$ 4. $5\overline{)40}$ 5. $3\overline{)27}$ 6. $5\overline{)25}$

7. $4\overline{)36}$ 8. $3\overline{)21}$ 9. $5\overline{)45}$ 10. $2\overline{)14}$ 11. $3\overline{)9}$ 12. $4\overline{)32}$

13. $5\overline{)15}$ 14. $4\overline{)24}$ 15. $2\overline{)16}$ 16. $5\overline{)20}$ 17. $4\overline{)16}$ 18. $4\overline{)28}$

19. $3\overline{)15}$ 20. $4\overline{)8}$ 21. $5\overline{)35}$ 22. $3\overline{)24}$ 23. $5\overline{)30}$ 24. $3\overline{)18}$

25. $20 \div 4 =$ ▨   26. $35 \div 5 =$ ▨   27. $45 \div 5 =$ ▨

28. $32 \div 4 =$ ▨   29. $20 \div 5 =$ ▨   30. $36 \div 4 =$ ▨

Look at this division.

$$\begin{array}{r} 6 \\ 4\overline{)24} \end{array}$$

★ 31. Which number is the dividend?

★ 32. Which number is the divisor?

★ 33. Which number is the quotient?

PROBLEM SOLVING

34. The coach has 30 baseball shirts. There are 5 in each box. How many boxes are there?

35. The coach had 28 baseballs. She gave 4 baseballs to the team. How many baseballs did she have left?

36. 30 people watched the baseball team practice. 5 people left before the practice was over. How many people watched the entire practice?

37. 36 students tried out for the baseball team. 4 students can fit on a bench. How many benches are needed for all the players?

Dividing by 6 or 7

Sam has 30 model cars.
He can put 6 in each case.
How many cases can he fill?

Divide: $6\overline{)30}$

■ × 6 = 30
5 × 6 = 30   **Just right!**

$6\overline{)30}^{\ 5}$

Sam can fill 5 cases.

TRY THESE

1. $6\overline{)6}$ ■ × 6 = 6

2. $6\overline{)12}$ ■ × 6 = 12

3. $6\overline{)18}$ ■ × 6 = 18

4. $6\overline{)24}$ ■ × 6 = 24

5. $6\overline{)30}$ ■ × 6 = 30

6. $6\overline{)36}$ ■ × 6 = 36

7. $6\overline{)42}$ ■ × 6 = 42

8. $6\overline{)48}$ ■ × 6 = 48

9. $6\overline{)54}$ ■ × 6 = 54

10. $7\overline{)7}$ ■ × 7 = 7

11. $7\overline{)14}$ ■ × 7 = 14

12. $7\overline{)21}$ ■ × 7 = 21

13. $7\overline{)28}$ ■ × 7 = 28

14. $7\overline{)35}$ ■ × 7 = 35

15. $7\overline{)42}$ ■ × 7 = 42

16. $7\overline{)49}$ ■ × 7 = 49

17. $7\overline{)56}$ ■ × 7 = 56

18. $7\overline{)63}$ ■ × 7 = 63

SKILLS PRACTICE

Divide.

1. $6\overline{)48}$ **2.** $7\overline{)49}$ **3.** $7\overline{)28}$ **4.** $4\overline{)32}$ **5.** $2\overline{)18}$ **6.** $6\overline{)36}$

7. $7\overline{)63}$ **8.** $6\overline{)42}$ **9.** $7\overline{)35}$ **10.** $3\overline{)24}$ **11.** $5\overline{)20}$ **12.** $6\overline{)24}$

13. $3\overline{)21}$ **14.** $5\overline{)45}$ **15.** $2\overline{)14}$ **16.** $5\overline{)35}$ **17.** $4\overline{)28}$ **18.** $7\overline{)21}$

19. $4\overline{)36}$ **20.** $6\overline{)12}$ **21.** $3\overline{)27}$ **22.** $6\overline{)54}$ **23.** $5\overline{)40}$ **24.** $7\overline{)42}$

25. $6\overline{)18}$ **26.** $4\overline{)24}$ **27.** $5\overline{)25}$ **28.** $7\overline{)56}$ **29.** $3\overline{)12}$ **30.** $6\overline{)30}$

31. $36 \div 6 = $ ▨   **32.** $63 \div 7 = $ ▨   **33.** $14 \div 7 = $ ▨

34. $12 \div 6 = $ ▨   **35.** $49 \div 7 = $ ▨   **36.** $54 \div 6 = $ ▨

Look at this division.

$$\begin{array}{r} 6 \\ 7\overline{)42} \end{array}$$

Match.

★ **37.** Divisor   **a.** 6

★ **38.** Dividend   **b.** 7

★ **39.** Quotient   **c.** 42

PROBLEM SOLVING

40. Janice has 28 toy trucks. She can put 7 in each garage. How many garages can she fill?

41. Janice put her 28 trucks on a track. Aaron put 4 of his trucks on the track. How many trucks are on the track?

42. Aaron has 7 trucks. Each truck has 8 wheels. How many wheels do these trucks have in all?

43. Janice has 48 barrels. Each truck can carry 6 barrels. How many trucks does Janice need to carry all the barrels?

Dividing by 8 or 9

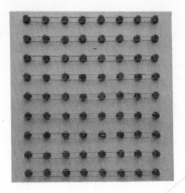
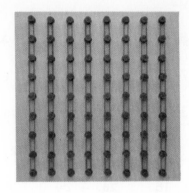

	sets		in each set		in all			sets		in each set		in all
	9	×	8	=	72			8	×	9	=	72

	72	÷	8	=	9			72	÷	9	=	8
	in all		in each set		sets			in all		in each set		sets

These multiplication and division facts form a *fact family.*

TRY THESE

1. $8\overline{)8}$ ■ × 8 = 8

2. $8\overline{)16}$ ■ × 8 = 16

3. $8\overline{)24}$ ■ × 8 = 24

4. $8\overline{)32}$ ■ × 8 = 32

5. $8\overline{)40}$ ■ × 8 = 40

6. $8\overline{)48}$ ■ × 8 = 48

7. $8\overline{)56}$ ■ × 8 = 56

8. $8\overline{)64}$ ■ × 8 = 64

9. $8\overline{)72}$ ■ × 8 = 72

10. $9\overline{)9}$ ■ × 9 = 9

11. $9\overline{)18}$ ■ × 9 = 18

12. $9\overline{)27}$ ■ × 9 = 27

13. $9\overline{)36}$ ■ × 9 = 36

14. $9\overline{)45}$ ■ × 9 = 45

15. $9\overline{)54}$ ■ × 9 = 54

16. $9\overline{)63}$ ■ × 9 = 63

17. $9\overline{)72}$ ■ × 9 = 72

18. $9\overline{)81}$ ■ × 9 = 81

SKILLS PRACTICE

Divide.

1. $8\overline{)40}$ 2. $9\overline{)63}$ 3. $8\overline{)64}$ 4. $9\overline{)36}$ 5. $7\overline{)56}$ 6. $8\overline{)72}$

7. $5\overline{)20}$ 8. $8\overline{)56}$ 9. $9\overline{)72}$ 10. $5\overline{)35}$ 11. $3\overline{)18}$ 12. $9\overline{)54}$

13. $9\overline{)27}$ 14. $4\overline{)28}$ 15. $6\overline{)54}$ 16. $9\overline{)81}$ 17. $8\overline{)32}$ 18. $7\overline{)49}$

19. $9\overline{)18}$ 20. $3\overline{)27}$ 21. $5\overline{)30}$ 22. $8\overline{)48}$ 23. $3\overline{)24}$ 24. $8\overline{)16}$

25. $7\overline{)35}$ 26. $8\overline{)24}$ 27. $4\overline{)16}$ 28. $3\overline{)15}$ 29. $6\overline{)36}$ 30. $9\overline{)45}$

★31. Write two multiplication facts and two division facts using the numbers 6, 7, and 42.

PROBLEM SOLVING

32. Sid had 54 nails. He wanted to put 6 nails in each row. How many rows could he fill?

33. Gail bought a package of 54 thumbtacks. She lost 6 of them. How many did she have left?

34. Gail bought 45 centimeters of wire. She cut it into pieces, each piece 9 centimeters long. How many pieces of wire did she have?

35. Peter bought 32 sheets of sandpaper. He put 4 sheets in each stack. How many stacks could he make?

EXTRA!   Relating Subtraction and Division

There are 24 baseball cards in a pack. 8 friends want to share the cards. Sally wrote this subtraction problem to find out how many cards each person would get. What division fact could she have used?

I subtracted 8 3 times. Each person will get 3 cards.

$$\begin{array}{r} 24 \\ -\ 8 \\ \hline 16 \\ -\ 8 \\ \hline 8 \\ -\ 8 \\ \hline 0 \end{array}$$

Division Properties

Divisor is 1

When you use 1 as the divisor, the quotient is the dividend.

$$4 \times 1 = 4$$
so $4 \div 1 = 4$

Divisor equals Dividend

When you divide a number by itself, the quotient is 1.

$$1 \times 6 = 6$$
so $6 \div 6 = 1$

Dividend is 0

When you use 0 as the dividend, the quotient is 0.

$$0 \times 5 = 0$$
so $0 \div 5 = 0$

A. Try this.

No number works.

$$\blacksquare \times 0 = 5$$
$$5 \div 0 = \blacksquare$$

B. Try this.

Any number works. There is no *one* right answer.

$$\blacksquare \times 0 = 0$$
$$0 \div 0 = \blacksquare$$

You cannot use 0 as a divisor.

TRY THESE

Can you do the division? If you can, give the quotient.

1. $6\overline{)0}$ 2. $0\overline{)6}$ 3. $1\overline{)7}$ 4. $0\overline{)8}$ 5. $8\overline{)0}$ 6. $9\overline{)9}$

SKILLS PRACTICE

Divide.

1. $6\overline{)42}$ 2. $5\overline{)0}$ 3. $3\overline{)18}$ 4. $1\overline{)7}$ 5. $4\overline{)20}$ 6. $3\overline{)15}$

7. $6\overline{)36}$ 8. $2\overline{)10}$ 9. $4\overline{)12}$ 10. $8\overline{)72}$ 11. $9\overline{)0}$ 12. $2\overline{)14}$

13. $3\overline{)3}$ 14. $5\overline{)45}$ 15. $4\overline{)0}$ 16. $6\overline{)54}$ 17. $3\overline{)27}$ 18. $9\overline{)72}$

19. $8\overline{)64}$ 20. $4\overline{)28}$ 21. $9\overline{)63}$ 22. $8\overline{)0}$ 23. $2\overline{)16}$ 24. $5\overline{)35}$

25. $5\overline{)25}$ 26. $1\overline{)0}$ 27. $6\overline{)24}$ 28. $8\overline{)32}$ 29. $9\overline{)45}$ 30. $6\overline{)48}$

31. $7\overline{)35}$ 32. $3\overline{)21}$ 33. $4\overline{)36}$ 34. $9\overline{)81}$ 35. $8\overline{)48}$ 36. $7\overline{)49}$

37. $24 \div 3 = \blacksquare$ 38. $18 \div 9 = \blacksquare$ 39. $5 \div 5 = \blacksquare$

40. $0 \div 2 = \blacksquare$ 41. $56 \div 8 = \blacksquare$ 42. $49 \div 7 = \blacksquare$

★43. $498 \div 1 = \blacksquare$ ★44. $0 \div 657 = \blacksquare$ ★45. $375 \div 375 = \blacksquare$

46. The divisor is 9. The dividend is 0. What is the quotient?

47. The divisor is 7. The dividend is 7. What is the quotient?

★48. Divide 671 by 671.   ★49. Divide 895 by 1.   ★50. Divide 0 by 396.

PROBLEM SOLVING

51. Inez had 4 skating caps. She gave 1 to Sue. How many did Inez have left?

52. Eric has 6 hockey pucks. He can put 6 pucks in 1 box. How many boxes does he need?

EXTRA! Using a Calculator
If you have a calculator, try this division problem.

$64 \div 0 = \blacksquare$

What does the calculator show?
If you don't have a calculator, can you guess what the calculator shows?

Division with Remainder

A. Pablo has 14 cups.
He puts 4 cups in each box.
How many boxes can he fill?
How many cups are left over?

He can fill 3 boxes.
There are 2 cups left over.

$$\begin{array}{r} 3 \text{ R2} \\ 4\overline{)14} \end{array}$$

R stands for **remainder**.
It tells how many are **left over**.

B. Find $3\overline{)19}$.

Draw 19 dots. Make sets of 3.

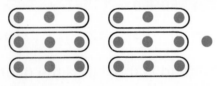

6 sets   1 dot left over

$$\begin{array}{r} 6 \text{ R1} \\ 3\overline{)19} \end{array}$$

C. Find $4\overline{)20}$.

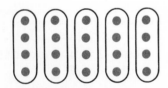

$$\begin{array}{r} 5 \text{ R0} \\ 4\overline{)20} \end{array}$$ or $$\begin{array}{r} 5 \\ 4\overline{)20} \end{array}$$

TRY THESE

Use the pictures to help you divide.

1. $3\overline{)14}$

2. $2\overline{)13}$

3. $4\overline{)16}$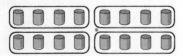

4. $5\overline{)14}$

SKILLS PRACTICE

Use the pictures to help you divide.

1. $6\overline{)17}$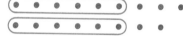

2. $5\overline{)15}$

3. $9\overline{)20}$

4. $3\overline{)17}$

Divide. Draw dots if necessary.

5. $2\overline{)7}$
6. $3\overline{)11}$
7. $5\overline{)16}$
8. $4\overline{)8}$
9. $6\overline{)13}$
10. $2\overline{)13}$

11. $4\overline{)14}$
12. $7\overline{)15}$
13. $6\overline{)18}$
14. $5\overline{)21}$
15. $3\overline{)19}$
16. $5\overline{)18}$

17. $8\overline{)20}$
18. $6\overline{)24}$
19. $9\overline{)24}$
20. $7\overline{)22}$
21. $4\overline{)17}$
22. $6\overline{)16}$

23. $3\overline{)7}$
24. $2\overline{)17}$
25. $8\overline{)11}$
26. $4\overline{)4}$
★27. $9\overline{)89}$
★28. $5\overline{)0}$

PROBLEM SOLVING

Draw dots if necessary.

29. Charles has 25 plates. He puts 8 in each stack. How many stacks can he make? How many plates are left over?

30. Sandy put 17 plates in the dishwasher. She broke 2 plates. How many plates does she have left?

31. Bev bought 24 glasses. They were shipped 6 in a box. How many boxes did she receive? How many glasses were left over?

★32. Five people are eating dinner at the table. Each person has a fork, a knife, and a spoon. How many pieces of silverware are on the table?

Long Division

George has 13 tennis balls.
He puts 3 balls in each can.
How many cans can he fill?
How many balls are left over?

$$3\overline{)13}$$

You do not need to draw dots.
Use multiplication to find how many cans he can fill.

Think: $\blacksquare \times 3 = 13$
$2 \times 3 = 6$
$3 \times 3 = 9$
$4 \times 3 = 12$
$5 \times 3 = 15$ Too Big!

He can fill 4 cans.

Now subtract to find how many balls are left over.

$$\begin{array}{r} 4\,R1 \\ 3\overline{)13} \\ \underline{12} \\ 1 \end{array}$$ ← $4 \times 3 = 12$

← left over

The remainder must be less than the divisor.
$1 < 3$

He can fill 4 cans. There is 1 ball left over.

TRY THESE

Use two ways to do each division.

1. $2\overline{)7}$ **2.** $3\overline{)14}$ **3.** $5\overline{)30}$ **4.** $4\overline{)29}$ **5.** $3\overline{)23}$ **6.** $4\overline{)18}$

SKILLS PRACTICE

Divide.

1. $2\overline{)11}$ 2. $4\overline{)14}$ 3. $5\overline{)41}$ 4. $3\overline{)13}$ 5. $4\overline{)30}$ 6. $3\overline{)17}$

7. $5\overline{)15}$ 8. $3\overline{)25}$ 9. $2\overline{)16}$ 10. $4\overline{)33}$ 11. $5\overline{)34}$ 12. $4\overline{)25}$

13. $4\overline{)27}$ 14. $5\overline{)49}$ 15. $2\overline{)15}$ 16. $4\overline{)12}$ 17. $3\overline{)28}$ 18. $5\overline{)42}$

19. $5\overline{)28}$ 20. $3\overline{)21}$ 21. $4\overline{)38}$ 22. $2\overline{)19}$ 23. $5\overline{)37}$ 24. $3\overline{)19}$

Look at this division.

$$\begin{array}{r} 6\ R2 \\ 3\overline{)20} \\ 18 \\ \hline 2 \end{array}$$

25. What is the divisor?

26. What is the dividend?

27. What is the quotient?

28. What is the remainder?

★ 29. The divisor is 3. What are the possible remainders?

★ 30. The divisor is 5. What are the possible remainders?

★ 31. Write this division another way. $5\overline{)30}^{\,6\ R0}$

PROBLEM SOLVING

32. The Sport Shop ordered 25 T-shirts. They were packed in boxes of 4. How many boxes did the Sport Shop receive? How many extra T-shirts were there?

33. The Sport Shop sold 25 pairs of socks. The socks come in packages of 3 pairs. How many packages did the Sport Shop sell? How many extra pairs were there?

117

Workbook   page 413

More Long Division

A. Carl picked 69 melons. He packed 7 melons in each crate. How many crates did he fill? How many melons were left over?

Divide: $7\overline{)69}$

Think:
$$\blacksquare \times 7 = 69$$
$$6 \times 7 = 42$$
$$7 \times 7 = 49$$
$$8 \times 7 = 56$$
$$9 \times 7 = 63$$
Use **9**.

$$
\begin{array}{r}
9 \text{ R6} \\
7\overline{)69} \\
63 \\
\hline
6
\end{array}
$$
$\leftarrow$ $\boxed{\mathbf{9 \times 7 = 63}}$

9 is the largest number to try.

Carl filled 9 crates. He had 6 melons left over.

B. Here is a way to check your division.

Multiply the divisor (7) and the quotient (9).

$$
\begin{array}{r}
7 \\
\times 9 \\
\hline
63
\end{array}
$$
$7 \leftarrow$ **melons in each crate**
$\times 9 \leftarrow$ **crates**

Add the remainder (6). The answer should equal the dividend (69).

$$
\begin{array}{r}
+\ 6 \\
\hline
69
\end{array}
$$
$+\ 6 \leftarrow$ **melons left over**
69 ✔ **melons in all**

TRY THESE

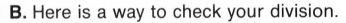

Use multiplication and addition to show that each exercise is correct.

1. $\begin{array}{r} 5 \text{ R3} \\ 7\overline{)38} \end{array}$
   2. $\begin{array}{r} 7 \text{ R1} \\ 6\overline{)43} \end{array}$
   3. $\begin{array}{r} 4 \text{ R7} \\ 8\overline{)39} \end{array}$
   4. $\begin{array}{r} 6 \\ 6\overline{)36} \end{array}$
   5. $\begin{array}{r} 6 \text{ R5} \\ 9\overline{)59} \end{array}$

Divide. Check your answers.

6. $8\overline{)73}$
   7. $7\overline{)57}$
   8. $9\overline{)35}$
   9. $6\overline{)42}$
   10. $7\overline{)67}$
   11. $6\overline{)59}$

SKILLS PRACTICE

Divide. Check your answers.

1. $7\overline{)20}$ 2. $6\overline{)44}$ 3. $3\overline{)21}$ 4. $8\overline{)45}$ 5. $4\overline{)37}$ 6. $3\overline{)20}$

7. $2\overline{)10}$ 8. $5\overline{)43}$ 9. $8\overline{)36}$ 10. $5\overline{)17}$ 11. $9\overline{)35}$ 12. $6\overline{)52}$

13. $7\overline{)54}$ 14. $8\overline{)9}$ 15. $3\overline{)27}$ 16. $6\overline{)56}$ 17. $2\overline{)7}$ 18. $7\overline{)22}$

19. $4\overline{)25}$ 20. $8\overline{)73}$ 21. $7\overline{)43}$ 22. $4\overline{)14}$ 23. $8\overline{)61}$ 24. $8\overline{)48}$

25. $6\overline{)46}$ 26. $9\overline{)86}$ 27. $5\overline{)39}$ 28. $6\overline{)36}$ 29. $9\overline{)89}$ 30. $9\overline{)69}$

PROBLEM SOLVING

31. Donna has 45 carrots. She wants to make bunches with 6 carrots in each bunch. How many bunches can she make? How many carrots will be left over?

32. Gail bought 38 bean plants. She put 5 plants in each box. How many boxes did she fill? How many plants were left over?

33. James picked 56 green peppers. He sold all but 8 of them. How many peppers did he sell?

★ 34. Mrs. Wilson picked 32 cucumbers. Mr. Wilson picked 45 cucumbers. How many cucumbers did the Wilsons pick? The Wilsons stored their cucumbers by putting 9 in each bag. How many bags did they fill? How many cucumbers were left over?

Problem Solving: Another Use of Division

READ   PLAN   DO   ANSWER   CHECK

A. You have used division to find *how many sets.*

13 fish in all
2 fish in each bowl

How many bowls?   6 bowls
How many fish left over?   1 fish left over

```
                    sets
                     ↓
                    6 R1 ←left over
in each set →2 ) 13 ←in all
```

B. This same division can be used to find *how many are in each set.*

13 fish in all
2 bowls
Same number of fish in each bowl.

How many fish in each bowl?   6 fish in each bowl
How many fish left over?   1 fish left over

```
            in each set
                ↓
                6 R1 ←left over
  sets → 2 ) 13 ← in all
```

TRY THESE

What must you find?   **A.** How many sets?   **B.** How many in each set?

1. 8 people went sailing. There were 2 boats. There were the same number of people in each boat. How many people were in each boat?

2. 8 people went sailing. 2 people went in each boat. How many boats were there?

3. Alice had 13 shells. She put 3 shells in each fish tank. How many fish tanks were there? How many shells were left over?

4. Alice had 13 shells. There were 3 fish tanks. She put the same number of shells in each tank. How many shells did she put in each tank? How many shells were left over?

PROBLEM SOLVING PRACTICE

Use the five steps to solve each problem.

1. 25 boats were tied to the docks. There were 5 docks. Each dock had the same number of boats. How many boats were tied to each dock?

2. The lighthouse has 120 steps. Amy has already climbed 87 steps. How many steps does she still need to climb?

3. The left side of a ship is called the *port* side. The right side is called the *starboard* side. 64 people sat on the port side and 89 people sat on the starboard side. How many people were on the ship?

4. Ellen won 19 fishing trophies. She kept her trophies in a cabinet with 3 shelves. She put the same number of trophies on each shelf. How many trophies did she put on each shelf? How many trophies were left over?

5. David put away 35 oars. Each cabinet held 8 oars. How many cabinets did he fill? How many oars were left over?

6. 32 people were in a boat race. There were 8 boats with the same number of people in each. How many people were in each boat?

7. Jenny photographed 9 sailboats last Saturday. Each sailboat held 7 people. How many people in boats did Jenny photograph last Saturday?

8. Peter bought 72 meters of rope. He needed to tie 8 boats to the dock. He wanted to use the same amount of rope for each. How much rope could he use for each?

★ 9. There were 80 boats with 1 mast and 52 boats with 2 masts. How many more boats had 1 mast?

★ 10. It is 14 km from marker 5 to marker 6. It is 19 km from marker 6 to marker 7. If a boat sails from marker 5 to marker 6 and then to marker 7, how many kilometers will the boat sail?

Problem Solving: Labeling Answers

You can use division to solve problems using money.

A. To find *how many*:

Karen had $35. She wanted to buy some teddy bears that cost $9 each. How many could she buy?

READ

Divide: $9\overline{)35}$

$$
\begin{array}{r}
3\ \text{R8} \\
9\overline{)35} \\
27 \\
\hline
8
\end{array}
$$

Karen could buy 3 bears.

$$
\begin{array}{r}
3 \\
\times 9 \\
\hline
27 \\
+\ 8 \\
\hline
35 \checkmark
\end{array}
$$

PLAN

DO

ANSWER

CHECK

B. To find *how much* each costs:

Mr. Maher sold $72 worth of animal puppets. He sold 8 puppets that each cost the same amount. How much did each cost?

Divide: $8\overline{)72}$

$$
\begin{array}{r}
9 \\
8\overline{)72} \\
72 \\
\hline
0
\end{array}
$$

Each puppet cost $9.

$$
\begin{array}{r}
9 \\
\times 8 \\
\hline
72 \checkmark
\end{array}
$$

TRY THESE

Would you *add*, *subtract*, *multiply*, or *divide* to solve these problems?

1. Jackie had $30. She spent $7 for a present. How much did she have left?

2. Jon had $26. He bought some games that cost $5 each. How many games could he buy?

3. Agnes bought 3 stuffed animals. They cost $7 each. How much did she spend?

4. Mark spent $20. He bought 4 presents. Each present cost the same amount. How much did each cost?

PROBLEM SOLVING PRACTICE

Use the five steps to solve each problem.

1. Michael bought 7 trucks and paid $8 for each one. How much did he spend?

2. Lee spent $32. He bought 4 electronic cars that each cost the same amount. How much did each cost?

3. Sara had $50. She bought some doll chairs that cost $8 each. How many chairs could she buy? How much did she have left over?

4. Tom has $22. Each present costs $4. How many presents can he buy? How much money will he have left?

5. Jerry had $7 and Nicky had $11. Who had more money? How much more?

6. A skateboard costs $20. A skating cap costs $4. How much do they cost in all?

7. An electronic game costs $25. Batteries cost $5. How much more does the game cost?

8. An electric train cost $56. Each of its 8 cars cost the same amount. How much did each car cost?

9. Peter bought 7 model cars. Each car cost the same amount. He spent $42. How much did each car cost?

★10. The Toy Store sold $54 worth of sleds between 3 and 4 o'clock. If the store sold 6 sleds, how much did each sled cost?

Make up a money problem for each.

★11. $48 \div 6 = $ ▨

★12. $6\overline{)37}$

✓Unit Checkup

Multiply. *(pages 88–95)*

1. 2
   $\times 7$

2. 5
   $\times 5$

3. 3
   $\times 9$

4. 6
   $\times 5$

5. 9
   $\times 6$

6. 7
   $\times 7$

7. 7
   $\times 6$

8. 8
   $\times 4$

9. 4
   $\times 3$

10. 7
    $\times 5$

11. 5
    $\times 2$

12. 4
    $\times 6$

13. 8
    $\times 7$

14. 4
    $\times 9$

15. $7 \times 6 = $ ▧

16. $5 \times 3 = $ ▧

17. $8 \times 9 = $ ▧

Complete the number sentences. *(pages 96–97)*

18. $3 \times 7 = $ ▧
    $7 \times 3 = $ ▧

19. $6 \times 8 = $ ▧
    $8 \times 6 = $ ▧

20. $4 \times 5 = $ ▧
    $5 \times 4 = $ ▧

21. $4 \times 1 = $ ▧

22. $7 \times 0 = $ ▧

23. $1 \times 1 = $ ▧

24. $1 \times 8 = $ ▧

25. $0 \times 3 = $ ▧

26. $0 \times 0 = $ ▧

Find the missing factors. *(pages 100–101)*

27. ▧ $\times 7 = 28$

28. ▧ $\times 9 = 54$

29. ▧ $\times 5 = 45$

30. ▧ $\times 3 = 24$

31. ▧ $\times 8 = 16$

32. ▧ $\times 6 = 30$

Divide. *(pages 104–111)*

33. $4\overline{)16}$

34. $7\overline{)21}$

35. $4\overline{)24}$

36. $8\overline{)48}$

37. $2\overline{)18}$

38. $8\overline{)72}$

39. $3\overline{)15}$

40. $5\overline{)45}$

41. $6\overline{)36}$

42. $9\overline{)72}$

43. $7\overline{)35}$

44. $9\overline{)63}$

45. $14 \div 2 = $ ▧

46. $42 \div 6 = $ ▧

47. $81 \div 9 = $ ▧

Complete the number sentences. *(pages 112–113)*

48. $0 \div 4 = $ ▧

49. $6 \div 6 = $ ▧

50. $9 \div 1 = $ ▧

51. $3 \div 3 = $ ▧

52. $0 \div 8 = $ ▧

53. $7 \div 1 = $ ▧

Find the quotients and remainders.   *(pages 114–119)*

54. $3\overline{)13}$ **55.** $5\overline{)23}$ **56.** $6\overline{)20}$ **57.** $4\overline{)18}$ **58.** $2\overline{)17}$ **59.** $4\overline{)28}$

60. $8\overline{)57}$ **61.** $5\overline{)13}$ **62.** $3\overline{)25}$ **63.** $2\overline{)7}$ **64.** $6\overline{)36}$ **65.** $6\overline{)45}$

66. $4\overline{)15}$ **67.** $2\overline{)12}$ **68.** $4\overline{)25}$ **69.** $8\overline{)38}$ **70.** $9\overline{)30}$ **71.** $5\overline{)42}$

72. $9\overline{)79}$ **73.** $5\overline{)25}$ **74.** $3\overline{)7}$ **75.** $9\overline{)46}$ **76.** $8\overline{)20}$ **77.** $6\overline{)50}$

Solve the problems. Draw pictures if needed.   *(pages 98–99, 120–123)*

78. There were 4 students. Each student did 6 jumping jacks. How many jumping jacks were done?   24

79. Jack put 4 weights on the weight-lifting bar. Each weight weighed 5 pounds. How much weight did he lift?

80. 15 students were using the balance beams. There were 5 students at each balance beam. How many balance beams were being used?   3

81. 16 students used the chin-up bar. There were 2 chin-up bars. The same number of students used each. How many students used each chin-up bar?

82. 60 students were in the gym. They formed teams with 8 students on each team. How many teams were formed? How many students were left over?

83. The coach had $50. He wanted to buy basketballs. Each basketball cost $8. How many balls could he buy? How much money did he have left?

84. Cathy sold $27 worth of hockey tickets. She sold 9 tickets. Each cost the same amount. How much did each cost? $3.00

85. Rene did 7 cartwheels in her routine. She practiced her routine 3 times. How many cartwheels did she do?

86. The coach bought 6 baseball bats. Each bat cost $8. What was the total cost? $48.00

87. 6 students did backflips. Each student did 6 backflips. How many backflips were done?

125

Reinforcement

More Help with Multiplication

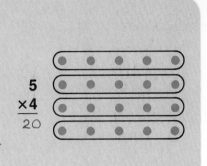

Multiply.

1. $\begin{array}{r} 6 \\ \times 2 \\ \hline \end{array}$	**2.** $\begin{array}{r} 3 \\ \times 5 \\ \hline \end{array}$	**3.** $\begin{array}{r} 7 \\ \times 4 \\ \hline \end{array}$	**4.** $\begin{array}{r} 5 \\ \times 8 \\ \hline \end{array}$	**5.** $\begin{array}{r} 6 \\ \times 6 \\ \hline \end{array}$
6. $\begin{array}{r} 1 \\ \times 8 \\ \hline \end{array}$	**7.** $\begin{array}{r} 8 \\ \times 3 \\ \hline \end{array}$	**8.** $\begin{array}{r} 0 \\ \times 4 \\ \hline \end{array}$	**9.** $\begin{array}{r} 6 \\ \times 7 \\ \hline \end{array}$	**10.** $\begin{array}{r} 7 \\ \times 3 \\ \hline \end{array}$
11. $\begin{array}{r} 6 \\ \times 5 \\ \hline \end{array}$	**12.** $\begin{array}{r} 9 \\ \times 9 \\ \hline \end{array}$	**13.** $\begin{array}{r} 8 \\ \times 4 \\ \hline \end{array}$	**14.** $\begin{array}{r} 8 \\ \times 8 \\ \hline \end{array}$	**15.** $\begin{array}{r} 7 \\ \times 8 \\ \hline \end{array}$

$\blacksquare \times 4 = 12$

$1 \times 4 = 4$ Too small.
$2 \times 4 = 8$ Too small.
$3 \times 4 = 12$ Just right!

Find the missing factors.

16. $\blacksquare \times 2 = 6$ **17.** $\blacksquare \times 7 = 14$

18. $\blacksquare \times 3 = 18$ **19.** $\blacksquare \times 4 = 16$

20. $\blacksquare \times 9 = 45$ **21.** $\blacksquare \times 9 = 54$

More Help with Division

$5 \times 2 = 10$

$2\overline{)10}$ with quotient 5

Divide.

22. $3\overline{)18}$ **23.** $2\overline{)8}$ **24.** $4\overline{)20}$ **25.** $4\overline{)32}$

26. $9\overline{)27}$ **27.** $5\overline{)30}$ **28.** $1\overline{)5}$ **29.** $7\overline{)35}$

30. $2\overline{)16}$ **31.** $8\overline{)8}$ **32.** $6\overline{)36}$ **33.** $8\overline{)64}$

34. $3\overline{)0}$ **35.** $7\overline{)49}$ **36.** $8\overline{)72}$ **37.** $9\overline{)81}$

$4\overline{)13}$ = 3 R1

Find the quotient and remainder.

38. $2\overline{)13}$ **39.** $3\overline{)17}$ **40.** $5\overline{)14}$ **41.** $4\overline{)18}$

42. $9\overline{)20}$ **43.** $7\overline{)23}$ **44.** $8\overline{)67}$ **45.** $3\overline{)22}$

46. $6\overline{)40}$ **47.** $5\overline{)27}$ **48.** $7\overline{)40}$ **49.** $9\overline{)59}$

A Special Number System

Suppose you could only use the numbers 1 to 7.
You count to 7 and then start again with 1.

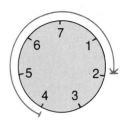

A. You could find sums in this number system.

$$4 + 5 = \begin{array}{r} 9 \\ -7 \\ \hline 2 \end{array}$$ No 9, so subtract 7.

In this system, 4 + 5 = 2.

$$2 + 3 = 5$$ You can use 5.

In this system, 2 + 3 = 5.

This addition table shows these sums. Copy and complete the table
for this number system. Describe the patterns you see in your table.

+	1	2	3	4	5	6	7
1							
2			5				
3							
4				2			
5							
6							6
7							

> Remember
> 7 is the largest
> number you can use.

B. You can also find products in this number system.

$$3 \times 6 = \begin{array}{r} 18 \\ -\ 7 \\ \hline 11 \\ -\ 7 \\ \hline 4 \end{array}$$

No 18, so subtract 7.

No 11, so subtract 7.

In this system, 3 × 6 = 4.

Make a multiplication table for this number system.
Describe the patterns you see in your table.

127

b Maintaining Skills

Choose the correct answer.

1. 395
    +224

    a. 171
    b. 619
    c. 519
    d. 629

2. 607
    − 89

    a. 518
    b. 528
    c. 682
    d. 511

3. 4,972
    +5,634

    a. 10,506
    b. 9,606
    c. 10,606
    d. 1,238

4. 95,005
    −43,394

    a. 52,711
    b. 51,611
    c. 52,611
    d. 51,601

5. $414.88
    − 195.09

    a. $219.89
    b. $229.79
    c. $381.81
    d. $219.79

6. $596.69
    +   24.24

    a. $620.93
    b. $572.45
    c. $610.93
    d. $620.83

7. 35,542
     3,679
    +24,311

    a. 63,532
    b. 53,532
    c. 62,532
    d. 63,530

8. 800,000
    − 97,563

    a. 897,563
    b. 802,437
    c. 702,437
    d. 713,547

9.   8
    ×6

    a. 14
    b. 48
    c. 56
    d. 40

10. $54 \div 6 = $ ▨

    a. 8
    b. 7
    c. 9
    d. 10

11. ▨ $\times 3 = 6$

    a. 18
    b. 2
    c. 3
    d. 9

12. $8\overline{)33}$

    a. 4
    b. 5 R1
    c. 4 R2
    d. 4 R1

13. Don does 9 chin-ups each day. How many chin-ups does he do in 7 days?

    a. 16 chin-ups   b. 63 chin-ups
    c. 2 chin-ups   d. 56 chin-ups

14. There were 32 students doing chin-ups. 8 students were using each chin-up bar. How many chin-up bars were there?

    a. 24 bars   b. 4 bars
    c. 40 bars   d. 5 bars

Money

A. You can use a cents sign (¢) or a dollar sign ($) to write about coins.

penny	nickel	dime	quarter	half-dollar
1¢ or $.01	5¢ or $.05	10¢ or $.10	25¢ or $.25	50¢ or $.50

B. You can also use a dollar sign ($) or a cents sign (¢) to write about bills.

one-dollar bill	five-dollar bill	ten-dollar bill
$1.00 or 100¢	$5.00 or 500¢	$10.00 or 1000¢

C. To find out how much money it is easiest to start by counting the bills and coins that are worth the most.

$1.00 + $.25 + $.10 + $.10 + $.05 + $.01 + $.01

| $1.00 | $1.25 | $1.35 | $1.45 | $1.50 | $1.51 | $1.52 |

TRY THESE

How much money?

1.  **2.**

3. 5 dollars, 3 dimes, 9 pennies

4. 3 dollars, 2 quarters, 1 nickel, 3 pennies

SKILLS PRACTICE

Use a dollar sign to show the amount.

1.

2.

3.

4.

5.

6.

7. 1 dollar, 3 quarters, 2 dimes

8. 2 quarters, 1 dime, 1 nickel, 4 pennies

9. 11 dollars, 5 dimes, 5 pennies

10. 2 dollars, 1 half dollar, 2 quarters, 1 dime

Find the total.

							Total
11.			1	1	2	3	
12.	1	1		2	1		
13.	4			1	1	1	
14.	1	3		2	4		1	
15.	1	2	1	1		3	
16.	2			3	1	3	

Which is worth more?

17. 3 nickels or 1 quarter

18. 1 dime and 1 nickel or 1 quarter

★19. 7 dimes or 5 dimes and 5 nickels

★20. 3 quarters and 2 dimes or 9 dimes

Problem Solving: Using Money

Sometimes you know the total value and must find what bills and coins to use.

A. Jan was at the toy store.
She spent a total of $3.55.
She gave the clerk $5.00.
The cash register showed that Jan should get back $1.45. What bills and coins should the clerk give Jan?

$$\begin{array}{r} \$5.00 \\ -\ 3.55 \\ \hline \$1.45 \end{array}$$

The clerk wants to use the largest bills and coins possible.

$1.00	+25¢	+10¢	+10¢

Count	**$1.00**	**$1.25**	**$1.35**	**$1.45**

The clerk should give Jan 1 dollar, 1 quarter, and 2 dimes.

B. Todd wanted to pay for a game that cost $2.60. Name the fewest bills and coins he could use to buy the game.

Think of the largest bills and coins Todd could use.

$1.00	+$1.00	+50¢	+10¢

Count	**$1.00**	**$2.00**	**$2.50**	**$2.60**

Todd could use 2 dollars, 1 half-dollar and 1 dime.

TRY THESE

Name the fewest bills and coins you could use to make each amount.

1. 15¢   **2.** 76¢   **3.** $1.25   **4.** $1.52   **5.** $2.16   **6.** $4.23

PROBLEM SOLVING PRACTICE

1. Ruth bought a teddy bear for her little brother. The cash register showed that she should get back $1.52. What bills and coins should the clerk give Ruth?

2. Sally bought a kite as a birthday present for John. The cash register showed that she should get back $3.85. What bills and coins should the clerk give Sally?

3. Lorenzo has 4 coins in his pocket. They make a total of 61¢. What 4 coins does Lorenzo have?

4. Larry is buying a skateboard for $4.30. What are the fewest bills and coins he could use to pay for the skateboard?

★ 5. The clerk is supposed to give Dan 26¢ in change, but there are no quarters in the cash register. What coins can she give Dan?

★ 6. Laura has 55¢ in her pockets. Name 3 ways to make this amount.

Copy and complete this table. Name the fewest bills and coins you could use to buy each item.

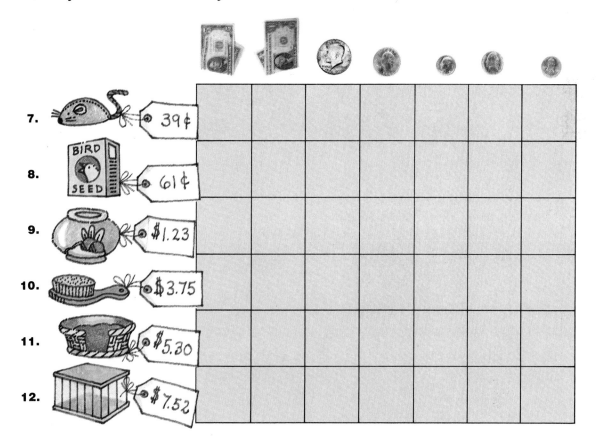

7. 39¢						
8. 61¢						
9. $1.23						
10. $3.75						
11. $5.30						
12. $7.52						

Problem Solving: Two-Step Problems

To solve these problems you must use two steps.

A. Donna bought a leash for $3.39 and a feeding dish for $2.45. She gave the clerk $10.00. How much should she get back?

Think: What Donna gets back is what she gave — what she spent.

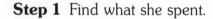

$10.00 $3.39 + $2.45

Step 1 Find what she spent.

leash	$3.39
dish	+ 2.45
spent	$5.84

Step 2 Find what she gets back.

gave	$10.00
spent	− 5.84
gets back	$ 4.16

Donna should get back $4.16.

B. Mr. Sanchez bought 3 toys for his cat. Each toy cost $2. He gave the clerk $20. How much should he get back?

Think: What he gets back is what he gave — what he spent.

$20   3 × $2

Step 1 Find what he spent.

for each	$2
bought	× 3
spent	$6

Step 2 Find what he gets back.

gave	$20
spent	− 6
gets back	$14

Mr. Sanchez should get back $14.

TRY THESE

Which problems require two steps? Solve all the problems.

1. Joe bought a kitten bell. It cost 59¢. Joe gave the clerk 75¢. How much should Joe get back?

2. Lara bought a canary cage for $15.95 and a bird bath for $4.75. She gave the clerk $30. How much should Lara get back?

3. Gerbils sell for $2.89 each. Ms. Roberts bought two and gave the clerk $10.00. How much should the clerk give back to Ms. Roberts?

4. Mr. Sanchez gave the clerk $5.00 to pay for a dog collar that costs $2.85. How much should the clerk give back to Mr. Sanchez?

PROBLEM SOLVING PRACTICE

Which problems require two steps? Solve all the problems.

1. A box of hamster food costs $1.19. Rebecca bought two boxes and gave the clerk $5.00. How much should she get back from the clerk?

2. Colored sand sells for $1.79 a bag. Jenny bought a bag for her new fish bowl. How much should she get back if she gives the clerk $2.00?

3. Dog sweaters cost $3.19 each. Ms. Burke gave the pet shop clerk $5.00 for a sweater for her poodle. How much should she get back?

4. John bought a flea collar for $7.50 and some dog soap for $3.79. He gave the clerk $15.00. How much should he get back?

5. Pat had $4.60 in bills and coins. He bought a toy bone for 83¢. How much money did he have left?

★6. Mr. Francis had $2.35 in bills and coins and a check for $12.60. He bought a record for $7.50. How much did he have left?

EXTRA! **Finding Value of Currency**
You will sometimes see these bills. Find out their names and values.

What is the total value of the bills shown?

Telling Time

A. These clocks show 5:40. You can read this time as minutes *past* the hour or minutes *to* the next hour.

40 minutes past 5

20 minutes to 6

B. There are 60 minutes in one hour.

The minute hand goes around the clock once in an hour.

There are 24 hours in a day.

The hour hand goes around the clock twice in one day.

Use A.M. to write times between 12:00 midnight and 12:00 noon.

Use P.M. to write times between 12:00 noon and 12:00 midnight.

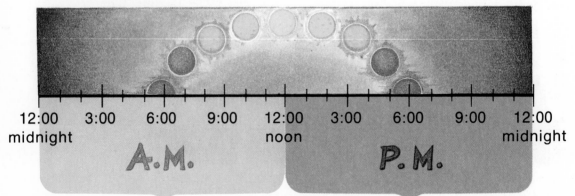

TRY THESE

Read each watch.

1.

███:███
███ minutes past ███

2.

███:███
███ minutes to ███

3.

███:███
███ minutes past ███

SKILLS PRACTICE

Read each clock.

1.

███:███
███ minutes past ███

2.

███:███
███ minutes past ███

3.

███:███
███ minutes to ███

4.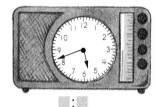

███:███
███ minutes to ███

5.

███:███
███ minutes to ███

6.

███:███
███ minutes past ███

Match the times.

7. 9:10   **a.** 15 minutes to 9

8. 8:50   **b.** 10 minutes past 9

9. 9:15   **c.** 15 minutes past 9

10. 8:45   **d.** 10 minutes to 9

Is it light or dark outside at:

11. 12:00 noon

12. 12:00 midnight

13. 2:30 A.M.

14. 2:30 P.M.

Use A.M. or P.M. to complete each sentence.

15. The sun rose at 6:30 _____.

16. The sun set at 6:30 _____.

17. Raul ate lunch at 11:45 _____.

18. Trisha ate lunch at 12:15 _____.

★19. The moon was bright at 10:30 _____.

★20. The moon was bright at 2:00 _____.

Problem Solving: Using Time

A. What time will it be 5 hours **after:**

3:00 P.M.

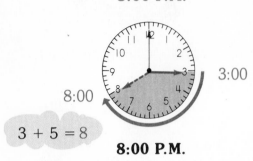

3:00

8:00

3 + 5 = 8

8:00 P.M.

11:00 A.M.

11:00

1 hour to noon

5 − 1 = 4

4:00

4:00 P.M.

B. What time was it 9 hours **before:**

10:00 P.M.

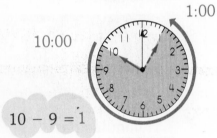

1:00

10:00

10 − 9 = 1

1:00 P.M.

9 − 4 = 5

4:00 P.M.

4 hours back to noon

4:00

7:00

7:00 A.M.

C. Find the number of hours **between:**

6:00 A.M. and 10:00 A.M.

10:00

6:00

4 hours

8:00 P.M. and 3:00 A.M.

4 hours to midnight

8:00

4 + 3 = 7

3:00

7 hours

TRY THESE

1. The bake shop in the Mid-City Mall opened at 9:00 A.M. The baker arrived 4 hours earlier to bake bread. When did the baker arrive?

2. Every Tuesday, the Mid-City Mall has a clown show that lasts 3 hours. The show starts at 2:00 P.M. When does it end?

3. John shopped from 1:00 P.M. until 4:00 P.M. in the Mid-City Mall. How long did he shop?

4. Nancy arrived at the mall at 10:00 A.M. She shopped until 3:00 P.M. How long did she shop?

PROBLEM SOLVING PRACTICE

1. The manager of the mall starts work at 9:00 A.M. He works for 8 hours. When does he finish?

2. The Mid-City Mall opens at 9:00 A.M. and closes at 8:00 P.M. How long is the mall open?

3. The delivery truck for Hall's Department Store left the mall at 10:00 A.M. It was gone for 7 hours. When did it return?

4. There was a traffic jam, so it took Jason 2 hours to reach the mall. He got to the mall at 1:00 P.M. When had he left home?

5. The Mid-City Mall Restaurant closes at 8:00 P.M. It opens at 7:00 A.M. How much time passes between closing and opening?

6. The dogs in the pet shop are fed at 9:00 A.M. and 6:00 P.M. How long must the dogs wait between the morning and evening meals?

★ 7. The sporting goods store in the mall is open 10 hours every day. It opens at 9:30 A.M. When does it close?

★ 8. Polly came to the mall at 10:00 A.M. She spent 2 hours shopping for clothes and 1 hour shopping for books. How long did she shop? When did she leave?

Workbook   page 417

restaurant
7:00 AM TO 8:00 PM

139

Problem Solving: More on Using Time

A. What time will it be 30 minutes **after**:

7:15 A.M.

7:45   7:15

$15 + 30 =$
45 after
7:00

7:45 A.M.

5:45 P.M.

15 minutes
to 6:00

$30 - 15 =$
15 after
6:00

5:45   6:15

6:15 P.M.

B. What time was it 45 minutes **before**:

2:00 P.M.

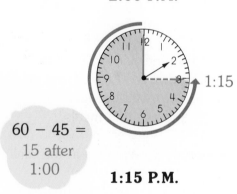

1:15

$60 - 45 =$
15 after
1:00

1:15 P.M.

4:15 P.M.

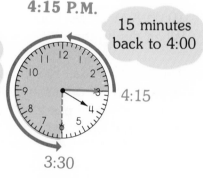

$45 - 15 =$
30 before
4:00

15 minutes
back to 4:00

4:15

3:30

3:30 P.M.

C. Find the number of minutes **between**:

2:15 P.M. and 2:45 P.M.

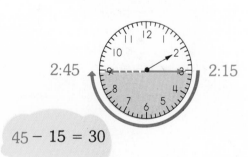

2:45   2:15

$45 - 15 = 30$

30 minutes

12:30 P.M. and 1:15 P.M.

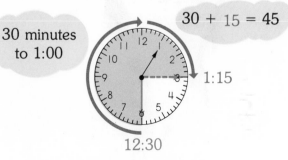

30 minutes
to 1:00

$30 + 15 = 45$

1:15

12:30

45 minutes

TRY THESE

1. Jamie started eating breakfast at 7:15 A.M. She ate for 30 minutes. When did she finish her breakfast?

2. Jamie started walking to school at 8:15 A.M. She arrived at 8:30 A.M. How long was her walk?

3. Jamie's class studied math from 9:45 A.M. until 10:30 A.M. How long did they study math?

4. Recess ended at 12:30 P.M. It was a 45 minute recess. When had recess begun?

PROBLEM SOLVING PRACTICE

1. Miko painted pictures from 1:00 P.M. until 1:30 P.M. How long did she paint?

2. John's class began singing at 1:30 P.M. They sang for 15 minutes. When did they finish singing?

3. John went outside to play at 3:45 P.M. He came inside at 4:30 P.M. because it had begun to rain. How long did he play outside?

4. Miko helped her father paint shelves for 45 minutes. They finished painting at 6:15 P.M. When had they begun?

5. Miko started playing the piano at 6:15 P.M. She practiced for 30 minutes. When did she finish?

6. John walked his dog from 7:30 P.M. to 7:45 P.M. How long did he walk the dog?

★ 7. Miko sat down to read at 7:00 P.M. She turned on the T.V. at 7:45 P.M. and watched until 8:30 P.M. How long did she watch T.V.?

★ 8. Miko began writing a letter to her grandmother at 8:30 P.M. She finished the letter at 9:00 and went to bed at 9:15. How long did it take her to write the letter?

a Maintaining Skills

Multiply.

1. 6
   ×5

2. 7
   ×3

3. 9
   ×4

4. 7
   ×8

5. 6
   ×1

6. 7
   ×7

7. 6
   ×8

8. 9
   ×6

9. 5
   ×8

10. 7
    ×6

11. 9
    ×8

12. 5
    ×7

13. 7
    ×4

14. 6
    ×6

15. 7
    ×9

16. 8
    ×8

17. 5
    ×9

18. 8
    ×3

19. 9
    ×9

20. 0
    ×7

21. 3
    ×9

Find the missing factors.

22. ▨ × 2 = 8

23. ▨ × 3 = 15

24. ▨ × 4 = 12

25. ▨ × 3 = 12

26. ▨ × 4 = 20

27. ▨ × 3 = 24

28. ▨ × 4 = 16

29. ▨ × 5 = 25

30. ▨ × 5 = 35

Divide.

31. 6)42

32. 4)36

33. 7)35

34. 6)38

35. 9)81

36. 4)29

37. 8)40

38. 6)54

39. 9)23

40. 6)25

41. 7)49

42. 8)66

43. 9)49

44. 8)48

45. 8)59

46. 1)6

47. 8)77

48. 9)63

Solve the problems.

49. 9 reporters work for the morning newspaper. 7 reporters work for the afternoon newspaper. How many reporters work in all?

50. A newspaper stand had 27 copies of the morning newspaper. It sold 9 copies. How many morning newspapers were left?

51. There were 8 reporters. Each reporter wrote 6 stories. How many stories did they write?

52. A newspaper bought new dictionaries for the reporters. Each dictionary cost $9. The total cost was $72. How many dictionaries were bought?

Project: Savings Account

Many people have a **savings account** at a bank. A **passbook** like this is used to show how much money has been deposited or withdrawn, and how much money is left.

	DATE	DEPOSIT	WITHDRAWAL	BALANCE
A.	NOV. 6	$15.00		$15.00
B.	NOV. 20	$ 6.75		$21.75
C.	NOV. 24		$5.25	$16.50

Read across each line of the passbook.

A. On November 6, Maria started her savings account by depositing $15.00. Her **balance,** the amount she had in the bank, was $15.00.

B. On November 20, Maria deposited $6.75. Her balance was then $15.00 + $6.75 or $21.75.

C. On November 24, Maria withdrew $5.25. Her balance was then $21.75 − $5.25 or $16.50.

Copy the passbook shown above. Continue the record to show the following deposits and withdrawals.

1. On November 30, a deposit of $4.25.
2. On December 5, a deposit of $6.89
3. On December 10, a withdrawal of $7.50.
4. On December 18, a withdrawal of $5.72.

How does a person open a savings account? How much money does a person need to open an account? Is the amount needed different for an adult than for a child?

Can you bank by mail? Who pays the postage?

CAREER

A **bank teller** must record deposits and withdrawals in savings accounts and checking accounts. Often, tellers use computers to help them in their work. Do you think bank tellers ever make mistakes?

Centimeter

A. The ***centimeter*** (cm) is a metric unit used to measure small lengths or distances.

The width of a paper clip is about 1 centimeter.

This ruler is marked in centimeters. The length of this pencil is 12 cm.

B. The length of this band-aid to the ***nearest centimeter*** is 7 cm.

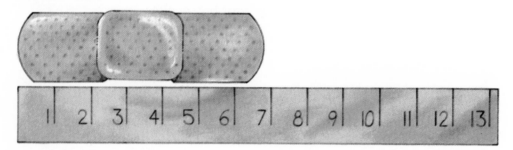

TRY THESE _____

Measure to the nearest centimeter.

1.

2.

3.

4.

5. Name some things you could measure in centimeters.

SKILLS PRACTICE

Measure to the nearest centimeter.

1.

2.

3.

4.

5.

6.

7.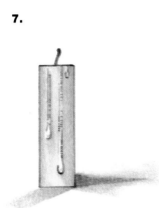

8.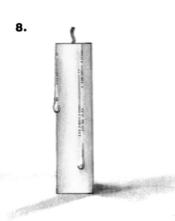

9.

Draw each.

10. a brick that is 15 cm long

11. a crayon that is 7 cm long

12. a nail that is 5 cm long

13. a jar that is 8 cm high

Estimate and then measure to the nearest centimeter.

14. the length of your shoe

15. the width of your shoe

16. the length of your thumb

17. the width of your thumbnail

★ 18. Name some things that are too small to measure in centimeters.

Meter and Kilometer

A. The *meter* (m) is another metric unit used to measure lengths or distances.

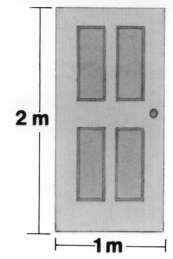

100 centimeters = 1 meter

The width of a door is about 1 m.
The height of a door is about 2 m.

B. The *kilometer* (km) is a metric unit used for longer lengths or distances.

1,000 meters = 1 kilometer

You can walk 1 km in about 10 minutes.
The distance from New York to Chicago is about 1,200 km.

TRY THESE

1. Name some things you could measure in meters; kilometers.

Estimate and then measure to the nearest meter.

2. the width of a window

3. the length of a bulletin board

4. the length of your classroom

5. the width of your classroom

SKILLS PRACTICE

Use cm, m, or km to complete each sentence.

1. A bed is about 2 _____ long.

2. A pen is about 14 _____ long.

3. The Mississippi River is 3,522 _____ long.

4. Mount Everest is about 9 _____ high.

5. The height of a stove is about 1 _____.

6. A basketball court is 30 _____ long.

7. A driveway is about 5 _____ wide.

8. A postcard is 14 _____ long.

Select the answer that seems reasonable.

9. The length of a car is about _____.
   a. 5 m   **b.** 50 m   **c.** 500 m

10. The height of Mount McKinley is about _____.
    a. 6 km   **b.** 60 km   **c.** 600 km

11. The length of a bar of soap is about _____.
    a. 1 cm   **b.** 10 cm   **c.** 100 cm

12. The length of a football field is about _____.
    a. 1 m   **b.** 10 m   **c.** 100 m

Copy and complete.

13. 1 meter = ▨ centimeters

14. 1 kilometer = ▨ meters

★ 15. 3 meters = ▨ centimeters

★ 16. 5 kilometers = ▨ meters

Other Metric Units

A. The *liter* (L) and *milliliter* (mL) are metric units used to measure liquid volume.

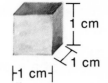

1 milliliter of water will fill a cube that is 1 cm long, 1 cm high, and 1 cm wide.

There is about 1 mL of liquid in an eyedropper.

1,000 milliliters = 1 liter

Milk is often sold in 1 L containers.

B. The *gram* (g) and *kilogram* (kg) are metric units of mass.

A paper clip has a mass of about 1 g.

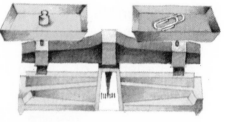

1,000 grams = 1 kilogram

This book has a mass of about 1 kg.

C. The *degree Celsius* (C°) is the metric unit used to measure temperature.

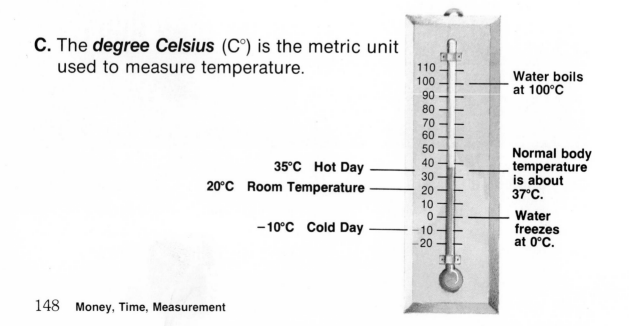

Water boils at 100°C

35°C Hot Day

Normal body temperature is about 37°C.

20°C Room Temperature

−10°C Cold Day

Water freezes at 0°C.

TRY THESE

1. Name some things whose volume you could measure in milliliters; liters.

2. Name some things whose masses you could measure in grams; kilograms.

3. Name some things you could do if the temperature outside were 36°C; −8°C.

SKILLS PRACTICE

Match to show which units you would use to measure:

1. mass of a person   **a.** kilograms
2. volume of water in a bathtub   **b.** grams
3. temperature of a room   **c.** liters
4. mass of a paper clip   **d.** degrees Celsius
5. volume of liquid in a bottle of perfume   **e.** milliliters

Use L, mL, g, or kg to complete each sentence.

6. A juice pitcher contains 1 _____ of juice.

7. An orange contains 50 _____ of juice.

8. A piece of popcorn has a mass of 1 _____.

9. A nine-year-old has a mass of about 35 _____.

Select the answer that seems reasonable.

10. An egg has a mass of about _____.
    a. 5 g   **b.** 50 g   **c.** 500 g

11. A telephone has a mass of about _____.
    a. 2 kg   **b.** 20 kg   **c.** 200 kg

12. A can of soup contains about _____ of soup.
    a. 3 mL   **b.** 30 mL   **c.** 300 mL

13. A car's gas tank contains about _____ of gas.
    a. 6 L   **b.** 60 L   **c.** 600 L

14. The temperature of very hot soup is about _____.
    a. −8°C   **b.** 8°C   **c.** 80°C

Copy and complete.

15. 1 liter = ▓ milliliters

16. 1 kilogram = ▓ grams

★ 17. 2 liters = ▓ milliliters

★ 18. 3 kilograms = ▓ grams

Problem Solving: Finding Needed Facts

Sometimes you need to find some facts in order to solve a problem.

A. The problem below does not contain all of the facts you need. Use the table to find the missing fact.

Anne bought a liter of milk.
She used 500 milliliters of milk.
How much milk did she have left?

> 1 meter = 100 centimeters
> 1 kilometer = 1,000 meters
> 1 liter = 1,000 milliliters
> 1 kilogram = 1,000 grams

Use the fact that 1 liter = 1,000 milliliters.

$$\begin{array}{r} 1{,}000 \\ -500 \\ \hline 500 \end{array}$$ Anne had 500 milliliters left.

B. Use the table below to find the missing fact.

Anne's family camped for 2 days on Gray Mountain and 1 day on Lang Mountain. Then they spent 1 week camping in the State Forest. How many days did they camp in all?

> 1 minute = 60 seconds
> 1 hour = 60 minutes
> 1 day = 24 hours
> 1 week = 7 days
> 1 year = 12 months

Use 1 week = 7 days to find how many days in all.

$2 + 1 + 7 = 10$ Anne's family camped for 10 days.

C. Sometimes a fact you need to solve a problem is not given.

Anne is 5 years older than Jim.
How old is Anne?

Before you can solve the problem you must find how old Jim is.

150 **Money, Time, Measurement**

TRY THESE _____

Write the fact you must find to solve each problem. Solve the problem.

1. Tom bought 1 meter of wire to hang a picture. He has 12 cm of wire left. How much wire did he use?

2. In the morning, Jay walked for 30 minutes. At night he walked for 1 hour. How many minutes did he walk in all?

PROBLEM SOLVING PRACTICE _____

What fact must you know to solve each problem? Solve the problem if you can.

1. Anne's family can drive to their cabin in 1 hour. They have already driven for 35 minutes. How much longer do they need to drive?

2. Anne can swim 1 kilometer. Her younger brother can only swim a short distance. How much farther can Anne swim?

3. Anne's family spends 3 months of the year in their cabin on the lake. They spend the rest of the year in their home in Dansville. How many months do they spend in Dansville?

4. Tom used 1 m of string to tie up a package. Then he used 20 cm of string to make a handle for the package. He also used 70 cm of string to tie up another package. How many centimeters of string did he use in all?

5. Anne mixed 1 liter of orange juice and 1 liter of grapefruit juice with some apple juice. How many milliliters of juice did she mix?

6. Tom bought 1 kilogram of apples. He ate an apple that had a mass of 85 grams. How many grams of apples did he have left?

7. Jason jumped 90 centimeters on his first jump. On his second jump, he jumped 1 meter. How much farther did he jump on his second jump?

8. Anne's friend Rosa came to visit. She stayed in the cabin for 1 week. Later in the summer, she stayed for 2 days. How many days in all did Rosa stay in the cabin?

★9. Jason used one liter of water to water two plants. He gave six hundred milliliters of water to one plant. How much water did he give the other plant?

★10. Tom swims for 2 hours every day. How many hours does he swim in a week?

Inch, Half-Inch, Quarter-Inch

A. The *inch* (in.) is a customary unit used to measure small lengths or distances.

A bottle cap is about 1 inch across.

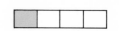
1 in.

1 inch

1 in.

1 half-inch

$\frac{1}{2}$ in.

1 quarter-inch

$\frac{1}{4}$ in.

B. You can use these rulers to measure to the *nearest inch, half-inch,* or *quarter-inch.*

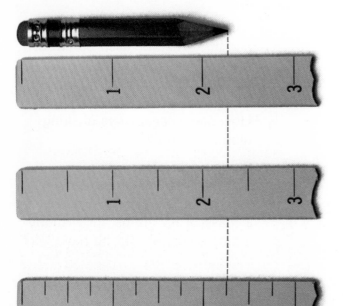

Using an inch ruler, length: 2 in.

Using a half-inch ruler, length: $2\frac{1}{2}$ in.

Using a quarter-inch ruler, length: $2\frac{1}{4}$ in.

TRY THESE

1. Name some things you could measure in inches.

2. Estimate and then measure the width of a page of this book to the nearest inch, half-inch, and quarter-inch.

Measure to the nearest inch.

1.

2.

Measure to the nearest half-inch.

3.

4.

Measure to the nearest quarter-inch.

5.

6.

Draw each.

7. a brick that is $6\frac{1}{2}$ in. long

8. a crayon that is $2\frac{1}{2}$ in. long

9. a nail that is $1\frac{1}{4}$ in. long

10. a jar that is 4 in. high

Estimate and then measure to the nearest half-inch.

11. the length of your shoe

12. the width of your shoe

13. the length of your thumb

14. the width of your thumbnail

★15. Name some things that are too small to measure in inches.

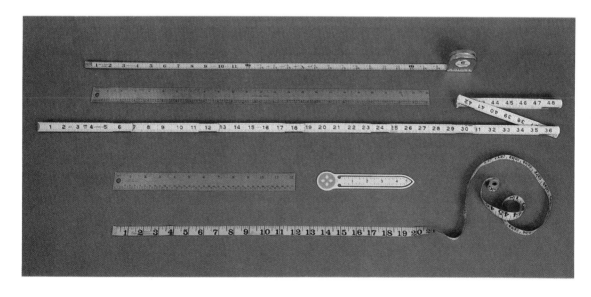

Foot, Yard, and Mile

The *foot* (ft), *yard* (yd), and *mile* (mi) are other customary units used to measure lengths or distances.

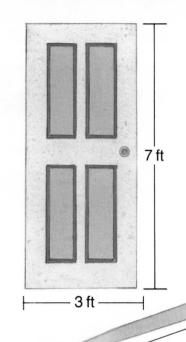

> **12 inches = 1 foot**
> **3 feet = 1 yard**
> **1,760 yards = 1 mile**

The width of a door is about 3 ft.
The height of a door is about 7 ft.

The length of a baseball bat is about 1 yd.

You can walk 1 mi in about 15 minutes.
The distance from Chicago to New York is about 750 mi.

TRY THESE

1. Name things you could measure in feet; yards; miles.

Estimate and then measure to the nearest foot.

2. the width of a window

3. the length of a bulletin board

Estimate and then measure to the nearest yard.

4. the length of your classroom

5. the width of your classroom

SKILLS PRACTICE

Use in., ft, yd, or mi to complete each sentence.

1. Your bed is about 6 ____ long.

2. A pen is about 7 ____ long.

3. The Mississippi River is 2,348 ____ long.

4. Mount Everest is about 5 ____ high.

Select the answer that seems reasonable.

5. The length of a car is about ____.
   a. 5 yd   **b.** 50 yd   **c.** 500 yd

6. The height of Mount McKinley is about ____.
   a. 4 mi   **b.** 40 mi   **c.** 400 mi

7. The length of a basketball court is about ____.
   a. 1 ft   **b.** 10 ft   **c.** 100 ft

8. The length of a baseball mitt is about ____.
   a. 1 in.   **b.** 10 in.   **c.** 100 in.

Copy and complete.

9. 1 foot = ▓ inches

10. 1 mile = ▓ yards

11. 1 yard = ▓ feet

★12. 4 feet = ▓ inches

★13. 2 miles = ▓ yards

★14. 5 yards = ▓ feet

PROBLEM SOLVING

15. Lisa knitted 1 foot of a scarf. She made a mistake and had to take out 3 inches. How many inches of scarf were left?

16. Lisa's mother knitted 1 yard of a scarf. Then she knitted 2 more feet to finish the scarf. How long was the finished scarf?

EXTRA! Drawing a Picture

An inch worm was crawling along a yardstick. It crawled 3 inches forward every hour and then slipped 2 inches back. How long did it take for the inch worm to reach the end of the yardstick?

Cup, Pint, Quart, and Gallon

The **cup, pint** (pt), **quart** (qt), and **gallon** (gal) are customary units used to measure liquid volume.

2 cups = 1 pint   **2 pints = 1 quart**   **4 quarts = 1 gallon**

  1 cup of water will fill a water glass.

Milk is often sold in 1 pt or 1 qt containers.

1 gal of paint will fill a large paint can.

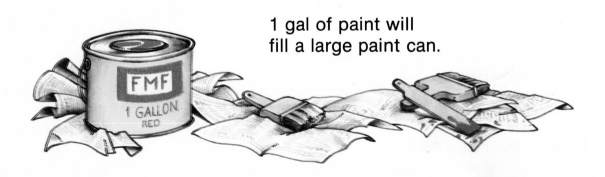

TRY THESE

1. Name some things whose volume you could measure in cups.

2. Name some things whose volume you could measure in gallons.

SKILLS PRACTICE

Use cup, pt, qt, or gal to complete each sentence.

1. The milk carton sold at your school contains 1 ____ of milk.

2. A wading pool contains about 200 ____ of water.

3. A large soup bowl contains about 1 ____ of soup.

4. A car's gas tank contains about 20 ____ of gas.

Select the answer that seems reasonable.

5. A bathtub contains about ____ of water.
   a. 2 gal   **b.** 20 gal   **c.** 200 gal

6. A can of soup contains about ____ of soup.
   a. 1 cup   **b.** 10 cups   **c.** 100 cups

7. A goldfish bowl contains about ____ of water.
   a. 1 pt   **b.** 10 pt   **c.** 100 pt

8. A juice pitcher contains about ____ of juice.
   a. 2 qt   **b.** 20 qt   **c.** 200 qt

Copy and complete.

9. 1 pint = ■ cups   10. 1 quart = ■ pints   11. 1 gallon = ■ quarts

★12. 3 pints = ■ cups   ★13. 4 quarts = ■ pints   ★14. 5 gallons = ■ quarts

PROBLEM SOLVING

15. Sam mixed 1 quart of orange juice, 1 quart of pineapple juice and 1 pint of grapefruit juice. How many pints of juice did he make?

16. Ramona bought 1 gallon of milk. She used 1 quart of milk to make yogurt. How much milk did she have left?

Upside-down answers 1. cup 5. c 9. 2

Workbook   page 421

157

Other Customary Units

A. The **_pound_** (lb) and **_ounce_** (oz) are customary units of weight.

A letter weighs about 1 oz.

An apple weighs about 3 oz.

> **16 ounces = 1 pound**

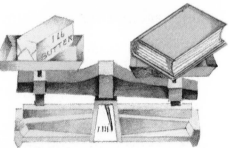

A package of butter weighs 1 lb.

This book weighs about 2 lb.

B. The **_degree Fahrenheit_** (°F) is the customary unit used to measure temperature.

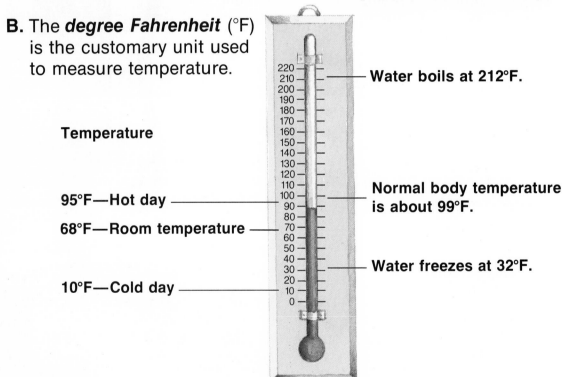

Temperature

95°F—Hot day

68°F—Room temperature

10°F—Cold day

Water boils at 212°F.

Normal body temperature is about 99°F.

Water freezes at 32°F.

TRY THESE

1. Name some things whose weight you could measure in ounces; pounds.

2. Name some things you could do if the temperature outside were 97°F; 5°F.

SKILLS PRACTICE

Match to show which units you would use to measure:

1. weight of a person   **a.** inches

2. length of a finger   **b.** cups

3. volume of water in a bathtub   **c.** miles

4. volume of water in a glass   **d.** degrees Fahrenheit

5. temperature of a room   **e.** ounces

6. distance from Denver to Detroit   **f.** gallons

7. the weight of a pencil   **g.** pounds

Use oz or lb to complete each sentence.

8. An egg weighs about 2 _____.

9. A nine-year-old weighs about 77 _____.

Select the answer that seems reasonable.

10. A piece of bread weighs about _____.
    a. 2 oz   **b.** 20 oz   **c.** 200 oz

11. A cat weighs about _____.
    a. 1 lb   **b.** 10 lb   **c.** 100 lb

12. The temperature of very hot soup is about _____.
    a. 2°F   **b.** 20°F   **c.** 200°F

Copy and complete.

13. 1 lb = ▨ oz

★ 14. 4 lb = ▨ oz

PROBLEM SOLVING

15. Jill bought 1 pound of butter. She used 4 ounces of butter to bake bread. How much butter did she have left?

16. Ramon bought 1 pound of potatoes. He cooked 10 ounces of potatoes. How many ounces of potatoes did he have left?

Count the money. *(pages 130–131)*

1.

2.

3.

4.

Read each clock. *(pages 136–137)*

5.

■:■
■ minutes past ■

6.

■:■
■ minutes to ■

7.

■:■
■ minutes to ■

Measure to the nearest centimeter. *(pages 144–145)*

8. ├─────────────┤

9. ├──────┤

10. ├────────────────────┤

11. ├──────────────────────────────┤

Match to show which metric units you would use to measure: *(pages 144–149)*

12. length of a soccer field	**a.** grams
13. volume of water in a bucket	**b.** liters
14. length of a tube of toothpaste	**c.** degrees Celsius
15. temperature of hot soup	**d.** kilometers
16. distance from Earth to Mars	**e.** centimeters
17. mass of a kangaroo	**f.** kilograms
18. mass of a pencil	**g.** meters
19. volume of medicine in a bottle	**h.** milliliters

Measure to the nearest half-inch. *(pages 152–153)*

20. |————————————|

21. |————————————|

22. |————|

23. |—————————————————————|

Match to show which customary units you would use to measure: *(pages 152–159)*

24. volume of water in a bathtub
25. distance from Hawaii to Puerto Rico
26. temperature of water in a bathtub
27. weight of an orange
28. length of a crayon
29. weight of a zebra
30. volume of soup in a soup bowl

a. ounces
b. cups
c. miles
d. gallons
e. inches
f. degrees Fahrenheit
g. pounds

Solve the problems. *(pages 132–135, 140–141, 150–151)*

31. Rosa spent $2.32 for invitations to her party. What are the fewest bills and coins she could use to pay?

32. Sam picked a package that contained 4 coins. They made a total of 41¢. What coins did the package contain?

33. Sharon bought Rosa a stuffed animal. It cost $2.29. She gave the clerk $5.00. How much should Sharon get back?

34. Rosa's party decorations cost $2.29 and paper napkins cost $1.48. She gave the clerk $4.00. How much should Rosa get back?

35. On the day of Rosa's party, Rosa's little brother stayed at his grandmother's house. He stayed from 10:00 A.M. to 6:00 P.M. How long did he stay?

36. Rosa's aunt came to help set up the party. She arrived 30 minutes before the party started. The party started at 2:00 P.M. When did Rosa's aunt arrive?

37. Rosa's party started at 2:00 P.M. and her guests stayed for 4 hours. When did the party end?

38. Rosa's guests started playing a game at 4:15 P.M. They finished at 5:00 P.M. How long did they play?

39. Rosa's mother bought 1 liter of milk. She used 800 milliliters of milk when she was baking for the party. How much milk does she have left?

40. Rosa's father can drive home from work in 1 hour. He has already driven for 45 minutes. How much longer does he need to drive?

Reinforcement

More Help with Money

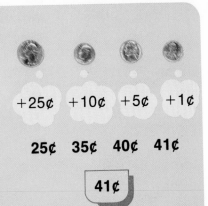

+25¢ +10¢ +5¢ +1¢

25¢ 35¢ 40¢ 41¢

41¢

Count the money.

1.

2.

3.

4.

5.

6.

More Help with Time

2:48
12 minutes to 3

7.

■:■
■ minutes past ■

8.

■:■
■ minutes to ■

9.

■:■
■ minutes to ■

10.

■:■
■ minutes to ■

11.

■:■
■ minutes past ■

12.

■:■
■ minutes to ■

Calendar Dates

A. A *calendar* names the days of the year as *dates*.
What is the date on the 40th day of the year?

        40 days
      −31 days in January
         9 days in February

The 40th day of the year is February 9.

B. What is the date 20 days after March 19?

    Through March 31: $31 - 19 = 12$
    Days left: $20 - 12 = 8$

The date is April 8.

Find the date 40 days after:

1. April 10

2. January 10

3. February 10

4. March 6

5. March 26

6. April 23

7. Every fourth year is a *leap year.* In a leap year, February has 29 days. Find the date 40 days after February 10 in a leap year. Compare your answer with the answer to Exercise 3.

JANUARY

	1	2	3	4	5	6
7	8	9	10	11	12	13
14	15	16	17	18	19	20
21	22	23	24	25	26	27
28	29	30	31			

FEBRUARY

				1	2	3
4	5	6	7	8	9	10
11	12	13	14	15	16	17
18	19	20	21	22	23	24
25	26	27	28			

MARCH

				1	2	3
4	5	6	7	8	9	10
11	12	13	14	15	16	17
18	19	20	21	22	23	24
25	26	27	28	29	30	31

APRIL

1	2	3	4	5	6	7
8	9	10	11	12	13	14
15	16	17	18	19	20	21
22	23	24	25	26	27	28
29	30					

MAY

		1	2	3	4	5
6	7	8	9	10	11	12
13	14	15	16	17	18	19
20	21	22	23	24	25	26
27	28	29	30	31		

JUNE

					1	2
3	4	5	6	7	8	9
10	11	12	13	14	15	16
17	18	19	20	21	22	23
24	25	26	27	28	29	30

Maintaining Skills

Choose the correct answer.

1. 9
   ×7

a. 36
b. 63
c. 54
d. not above

2. 7
   ×8

a. 56
b. 64
c. 65
d. not above

3. 6
   ×9

a. 63
b. 45
c. 56
d. not above

4. 8
   ×8

a. 46
b. 72
c. 64
d. not above

5. 89
   +77

a. 162
b. 156
c. 166
d. not above

6. 976
   +305

a. 1,291
b. 1,281
c. 1,271
d. not above

7. 809
   + 96

a. 893
b. 950
c. 905
d. not above

8. 6,729
   +5,976

a. 12,703
b. 12,730
c. 12,693
d. not above

9. 76
   +65

a. 114
b. 141
c. 131
d. not above

10. 798
   + 83

a. 881
b. 818
c. 871
d. not above

11. $59.76
   + 7.85

a. $66.61
b. $67.16
c. $67.61
d. not above

12. $91.72
   + 86.29

a. $178.97
b. $177.91
c. $178.01
d. not above

13. James was in the school orchestra. He practiced on his flute from 11:00 A.M. to 2:00 P.M. How long did James practice?

a. 9 hours
b. 3 hours
c. 13 hours
d. not above

14. The school band bought a new drum that cost $67.58. They also bought a new violin that cost $55.63. How much did the new musical instruments cost?

a. $123.12
b. $123.11
c. $122.11
d. not above

Multiplying by Ones 6

Multiplying 2-digit Numbers

A. Sandy bought 3 boxes of eggs.
There were 12 eggs in each box.
How many eggs did she buy?

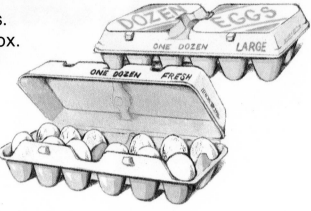

There are the same number of eggs in each box.
You can multiply to find how many eggs in all.

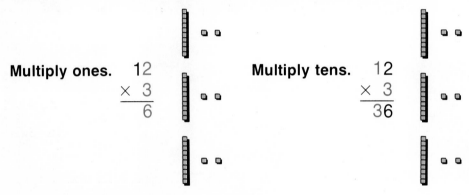

Multiply ones.

$$\begin{array}{r} 12 \\ \times\ 3 \\ \hline 6 \end{array}$$

Multiply tens.

$$\begin{array}{r} 12 \\ \times\ 3 \\ \hline 36 \end{array}$$

Sandy bought 36 eggs.

B. Find

$$\begin{array}{r} 2 \\ \times 43 \\ \hline \end{array}$$

When you change the order of the factors, you do not change the product.

Do

$$\begin{array}{r} 43 \\ \times\ 2 \\ \hline 86 \end{array}$$

TRY THESE

Multiply.

1. $\begin{array}{r} 12 \\ \times\ 2 \\ \hline \end{array}$
2. $\begin{array}{r} 21 \\ \times\ 4 \\ \hline \end{array}$
3. $\begin{array}{r} 10 \\ \times\ 3 \\ \hline \end{array}$
4. $\begin{array}{r} 11 \\ \times\ 5 \\ \hline \end{array}$
5. $\begin{array}{r} 20 \\ \times\ 3 \\ \hline \end{array}$
6. $\begin{array}{r} 2 \\ \times 23 \\ \hline \end{array}$

7. $3 \times 21 =$ ▓

8. $8 \times 11 =$ ▓

9. $41 \times 2 =$ ▓

SKILLS PRACTICE

Multiply.

1. 34
   × 2

2. 23
   × 3

3. 13
   × 2

4. 10
   × 4

5. 11
   × 7

6. 30
   × 3

7. 46
   × 1

8. 73
   × 0

9. 24
   × 2

10. 44
    × 2

11. 10
    × 8

12. 31
    × 3

13. 30
    × 2

14. 31
    × 2

15. 10
    × 2

16. 11
    × 9

17. 33
    × 2

18. 20
    × 2

19. 14
    × 2

20. 11
    × 6

21. 32
    × 3

22. 3
    ×22

23. 3
    ×13

24. 40
    × 2

25. 43
    × 2

26. 33
    × 3

27. 4
    ×11

28. 10
    × 5

29. 2
    ×41

30. 32
    × 2

31. 4 × 22 = ▧

32. 3 × 12 = ▧

33. 2 × 21 = ▧

34. 9 × 10 = ▧

35. 2 × 42 = ▧

36. 4 × 20 = ▧

37. 22 × 2 = ▧

38. 10 × 6 = ▧

39. 32 × 3 = ▧

PROBLEM SOLVING

> 1 dozen = 12

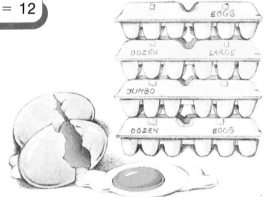

40. Sandy and her father went shopping together. They bought 1 dozen rolls at the bakery. How many rolls did they buy?

41. They bought 3 dozen apples at Mr. Ramon's farm stand. How many apples did they buy?

42. On the way home, they stopped at the flower store and bought 2 dozen roses. How many roses did they buy?

★ 43. They bought 4 dozen eggs. How many eggs did they buy? 2 eggs were broken. How many eggs were not broken?

Multiplying with Saving

A. Sometimes you must regroup 10 ones as 1 ten and **save** 1 ten.

Multiply ones.

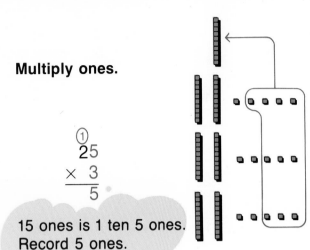

$$\begin{array}{r} \overset{①}{2}5 \\ \times\ 3 \\ \hline 5 \end{array}$$

15 ones is 1 ten 5 ones.
Record 5 ones.
Save 1 ten.

Multiply tens.
Then add the
1 ten you **saved.**

$$\begin{array}{r} \overset{①}{2}5 \\ \times\ 3 \\ \hline 75 \end{array}$$

B. Sometimes you must **save** more than 1 ten.

Multiply ones.

$$\begin{array}{r} \overset{②}{1}8 \\ \times\ 3 \\ \hline 4 \end{array}$$

24 ones is 2 tens 4 ones.
Record 4 ones.
Save 2 tens.

Multiply tens.
Then add the
2 tens you **saved.**

$$\begin{array}{r} \overset{②}{1}8 \\ \times\ 3 \\ \hline 54 \end{array}$$

TRY THESE

Multiply.

1. $\begin{array}{r} 26 \\ \times\ 3 \\ \hline \end{array}$
2. $\begin{array}{r} 12 \\ \times\ 6 \\ \hline \end{array}$
3. $\begin{array}{r} 35 \\ \times\ 2 \\ \hline \end{array}$
4. $\begin{array}{r} 18 \\ \times\ 4 \\ \hline \end{array}$
5. $\begin{array}{r} 28 \\ \times\ 3 \\ \hline \end{array}$
6. $\begin{array}{r} 3 \\ \times 17 \\ \hline \end{array}$

7. $2 \times 19 = $ ▨

8. $3 \times 28 = $ ▨

9. $49 \times 2 = $ ▨

Multiply.

1. 23 × 4	2. 13 × 7	3. 26 × 2	4. 12 × 3	5. 47 × 2	6. 33 × 3
7. 33 × 3	8. 19 × 3	9. 17 × 0	10. 29 × 2	11. 40 × 2	12. 14 × 6
13. 11 × 7	14. 48 × 2	15. 22 × 4	16. 57 × 1	17. 37 × 2	18. 19 × 5
19. 23 × 2	20. 15 × 6	21. 10 × 5	22. 16 × 6	23. 43 × 2	24. 18 × 5
25. 17 × 3	26. 24 × 2	27. 3 × 15	28. 34 × 2	29. 4 × 19	30. 24 × 4

31. $2 \times 28 = $ ▥

32. $8 \times 12 = $ ▥

33. $2 \times 32 = $ ▥

34. $3 \times 27 = $ ▥

35. $2 \times 34 = $ ▥

36. $2 \times 39 = $ ▥

37. $16 \times 4 = $ ▥

38. $14 \times 5 = $ ▥

39. $24 \times 3 = $ ▥

PROBLEM SOLVING

40. A bus tour visited the Grand Canyon. 27 people went down into the canyon. Each person carried 2 sandwiches. How many sandwiches did the people carry?

★ 41. A tourist used 3 rolls of film on the first day and 2 rolls on the second day. Each roll had 16 pictures. How many pictures did he take on the first day? On the second day? In all?

Larger Products

A. The new park has 52 light posts.
Each light will use 3 light bulbs.
How many light bulbs will be used?

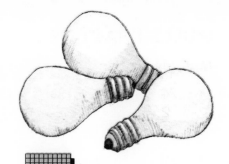

Multiply ones.

```
  52
×  3
----
   6
```

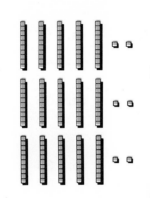

Multiply tens.

```
  52
×  3
----
 156
```

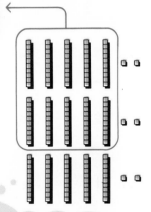

156 light bulbs will be used.

15 tens is 1 hundred 5 tens.
No need to save 1 hundred.
Record 15.

B. 7 × 29 = ■

Multiply ones.

```
    ⑥
   29
 ×  7
 ----
    3
```

Record 3 ones. Save 6 tens.

Multiply tens.
Add the 6 tens
you saved.

```
    ⑥
   29
 ×  7
 ----
  203
```

20 tens is 2 hundreds 0 tens.

TRY THESE

Multiply.

1.
```
  92
×  3
```

2.
```
  41
×  6
```

3.
```
  26
×  3
```

4.
```
  80
×  7
```

5.
```
  15
×  6
```

6.
```
  64
×  7
```

7. 3 × 27 = ▨

8. 4 × 81 = ▨

9. 38 × 6 = ▨

Multiply.

1. 74
   × 2

2. 41
   × 9

3. 71
   × 5

4. 50
   × 3

5. 43
   × 4

6. 32
   × 5

7. 10
   × 8

8. 63
   × 3

9. 72
   × 8

10. 21
    × 3

11. 61
    × 8

12. 56
    × 7

13. 11
    × 6

14. 38
    × 8

15. 47
    × 0

16. 67
    × 9

17. 60
    × 8

18. 16
    × 6

19. 85
    × 4

20. 26
    × 3

21. 20
    × 6

22. 94
    × 2

23. 84
    × 2

24. 24
    × 4

25. 56
    × 9

26. 82
    × 5

27. 8
    ×49

28. 68
    × 7

29. 74
    × 9

30. 8
    ×23

31. $3 \times 19 =$ ▨

32. $3 \times 54 =$ ▨

33. $7 \times 41 =$ ▨

34. $6 \times 95 =$ ▨

35. $3 \times 72 =$ ▨

36. $9 \times 24 =$ ▨

37. $15 \times 8 =$ ▨

38. $51 \times 4 =$ ▨

39. $97 \times 9 =$ ▨

PROBLEM SOLVING _____

Follow the instructions to reach the soccer field.

40. Start with 46.

41. Multiply by 9.

42. Add 76.

43. Subtract 418.

44. Divide by 8.

Follow the instructions to return.

49. Add 43.

48. Divide by 9.

47. Subtract 36.

46. Multiply by 7.

45. Start with 9.

ⓐ Maintaining Skills

Add, subtract, or multiply.

1. 6 +8	**2.** 15 − 8	**3.** 4 ×5	**4.** 12 − 7	**5.** 4 +6	**6.** 9 +8	**7.** 6 ×7

8. 5 ×3	**9.** 8 ×4	**10.** 16 − 9	**11.** 8 +3	**12.** 13 − 7	**13.** 3 ×8	**14.** 10 − 6

15. 9 +9	**16.** 5 ×6	**17.** 8 −3	**18.** 7 ×9	**19.** 3 +2	**20.** 18 − 9	**21.** 6 +5

Round to the nearest ten.

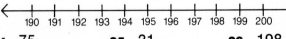

22. 194   **23.** 285   **24.** 75   **25.** 31   **26.** 198

Round to the nearest hundred.

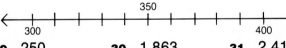

27. 304   **28.** 536   **29.** 250   **30.** 1,863   **31.** 2,414

Round to the nearest dollar.

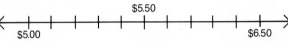

32. $5.29   **33.** $3.78   **34.** $2.50   **35.** $7.17   **36.** $6.83

Add or subtract.

37. 57 +38	**38.** 72 −55	**39.** 461 +239	**40.** 935 −257	**41.** 6,492 +5,318

42. 17,623 − 6,844	**43.** 56,731 +39,649	**44.** 18,995 +27,237	**45.** 40,000 − 7,234	**46.** 75,384 −29,699

Solve the problems.

47. An electrician had 72 feet of wire. She used 39 feet of it. How many feet of wire did she have left?

48. The electrician worked for 8 hours. Then she worked 3 hours overtime. How many hours did she work in all?

Project: Reading a Map

This map shows some of the roads in Iowa. Each small red numeral tells the distance in miles between a pair of red stars. The symbol in the upper-right corner of the map shows North, South, East, and West.

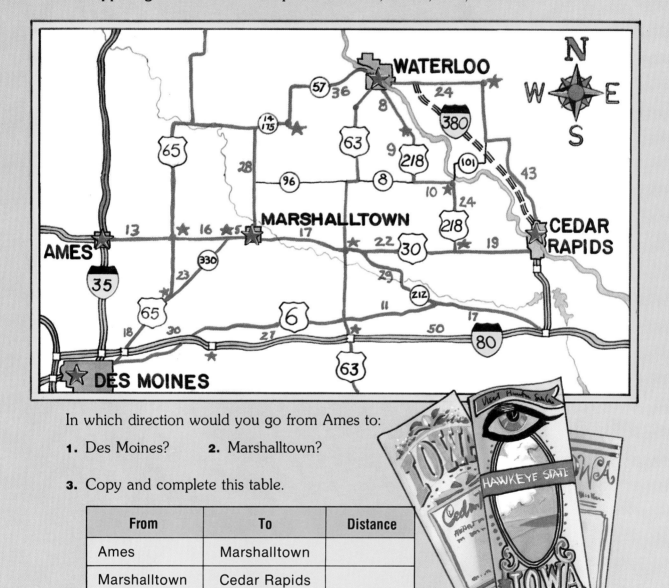

In which direction would you go from Ames to:

1. Des Moines?   **2.** Marshalltown?

3. Copy and complete this table.

From	To	Distance
Ames	Marshalltown	
Marshalltown	Cedar Rapids	
Cedar Rapids	Waterloo	

Look at a road map of your state. Choose three cities that you would like to visit. How far would you travel if you started in your home town, visited these three cities, and returned home?

Multiplying 3-digit Numbers

A. Mr. Jones bought 4 boxes of tiles.
There were 216 tiles in each box.
How many tiles did Mr. Jones buy?

Multiply ones.
②
216
× 4
―――
4

Multiply tens.
Add the 2 tens
you saved.
②
216
× 4
―――
64

Multiply hundreds.
②
216
× 4
―――
864

Mr. Jones bought 864 tiles.

B. Find 248 × 3.

Multiply ones.
②
248
× 3
―――
4

Multiply tens.
Add the 2 tens
you saved.
①②
248
× 3
―――
44

Multiply hundreds.
Add the
1 hundred
you saved.
①②
248
× 3
―――
744

TRY THESE ―――――――――――――――――――――

Multiply.

1.	2.	3.	4.	5.	6.
122 × 4	147 × 6	309 × 3	156 × 6	294 × 3	2 ×142

7. 3 × 319 = ▨

8. 4 × 102 = ▨

9. 156 × 6 = ▨

SKILLS PRACTICE

Multiply.

1. 275
   × 3

2. 186
   × 3

3. 192
   × 3

4. 114
   × 4

5. 244
   × 2

6. 150
   × 5

7. 413
   × 2

8. 148
   × 5

9. 127
   × 7

10. 118
    × 6

11. 323
    × 3

12. 319
    × 3

13. 124
    × 4

14. 3
    ×210

15. 286
    × 2

16. 197
    × 3

17. 338
    × 1

18. 239
    × 4

19. 216
    × 3

20. 418
    × 2

21. 207
    × 4

22. 143
    × 4

23. 108
    × 9

24. 264
    × 3

25. 3 × 281 = ▨

26. 6 × 162 = ▨

27. 4 × 215 = ▨

28. 273 × 2 = ▨

29. 184 × 5 = ▨

30. 265 × 3 = ▨

Find the missing numbers.

★ 31. 10⑧
       × 7
      ─────
       756

★ 32. 32⑦
       × 3
      ─────
       9▨1

★ 33. 1⑭6
       × 3
      ─────
       4▨8

PROBLEM SOLVING

34. An electrician wired 4 rooms. Each room needed 105 meters of wire. How much wire was used?

35. A work crew is building a driveway. The driveway is already 12 meters long. If the crew makes it 5 meters longer, how long will it be?

36. An electrician put 24 electrical outlets in a new house. Each outlet cost $6. How much did all the outlets cost?

★ 37. Mr. Davis is covering the floor with tiles. Each tile is 12 centimeters wide and costs $2. He used 48 tiles. How much did the tiles cost?

Larger Products

A. The Speedy Car Company makes 321 cars in one day. How many cars are made in 4 days?

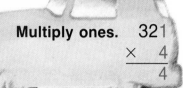

Multiply ones.
$$\begin{array}{r} 321 \\ \times\ \ 4 \\ \hline 4 \end{array}$$

Multiply tens.
$$\begin{array}{r} 321 \\ \times\ \ 4 \\ \hline 84 \end{array}$$

Multiply hundreds.
$$\begin{array}{r} 321 \\ \times\ \ 4 \\ \hline 1{,}284 \end{array}$$

12 hundreds is 1 thousand 2 hundreds. No need to save 1 thousand.

1,284 cars are made.

B. $284 \times 7 =$ ▨

Multiply ones.
$$\begin{array}{r} \overset{2}{2}84 \\ \times\ \ 7 \\ \hline 8 \end{array}$$

Multiply tens. Add the 2 tens you saved.
$$\begin{array}{r} \overset{5}{\overset{}{2}}\overset{2}{8}4 \\ \times\ \ 7 \\ \hline 88 \end{array}$$

Multiply hundreds. Add the 5 hundreds you saved.
$$\begin{array}{r} \overset{5}{\overset{}{2}}\overset{2}{8}4 \\ \times\ \ 7 \\ \hline 1{,}988 \end{array}$$

TRY THESE

Multiply.

1.
$$\begin{array}{r} 411 \\ \times\ \ 6 \end{array}$$

2.
$$\begin{array}{r} 177 \\ \times\ \ 4 \end{array}$$

3.
$$\begin{array}{r} 486 \\ \times\ \ 3 \end{array}$$

4.
$$\begin{array}{r} 530 \\ \times\ \ 7 \end{array}$$

5.
$$\begin{array}{r} 761 \\ \times\ \ 8 \end{array}$$

6.
$$\begin{array}{r} 5 \\ \times 826 \end{array}$$

SKILLS PRACTICE

Multiply.

1. $\begin{array}{r} 155 \\ \times\ \ 6 \\ \hline \end{array}$
2. $\begin{array}{r} 574 \\ \times\ \ 8 \\ \hline \end{array}$
3. $\begin{array}{r} 473 \\ \times\ \ 5 \\ \hline \end{array}$
4. $\begin{array}{r} 641 \\ \times\ \ 7 \\ \hline \end{array}$
5. $\begin{array}{r} 856 \\ \times\ \ 4 \\ \hline \end{array}$
6. $\begin{array}{r} 407 \\ \times\ \ 3 \\ \hline \end{array}$

7. $\begin{array}{r} 265 \\ \times\ \ 9 \\ \hline \end{array}$
8. $\begin{array}{r} 861 \\ \times\ \ 7 \\ \hline \end{array}$
9. $\begin{array}{r} 304 \\ \times\ \ 2 \\ \hline \end{array}$
10. $\begin{array}{r} 349 \\ \times\ \ 6 \\ \hline \end{array}$
11. $\begin{array}{r} 9 \\ \times 743 \\ \hline \end{array}$
12. $\begin{array}{r} 512 \\ \times\ \ 6 \\ \hline \end{array}$

13. $\begin{array}{r} 410 \\ \times\ \ 8 \\ \hline \end{array}$
14. $\begin{array}{r} 675 \\ \times\ \ 5 \\ \hline \end{array}$
15. $\begin{array}{r} 942 \\ \times\ \ 8 \\ \hline \end{array}$
16. $\begin{array}{r} 613 \\ \times\ \ 6 \\ \hline \end{array}$
17. $\begin{array}{r} 249 \\ \times\ \ 5 \\ \hline \end{array}$
18. $\begin{array}{r} 4 \\ \times 631 \\ \hline \end{array}$

19. $\begin{array}{r} 154 \\ \times\ \ 6 \\ \hline \end{array}$
20. $\begin{array}{r} 367 \\ \times\ \ 7 \\ \hline \end{array}$
21. $\begin{array}{r} 462 \\ \times\ \ 3 \\ \hline \end{array}$
22. $\begin{array}{r} 829 \\ \times\ \ 6 \\ \hline \end{array}$
23. $\begin{array}{r} 587 \\ \times\ \ 3 \\ \hline \end{array}$
24. $\begin{array}{r} 743 \\ \times\ \ 3 \\ \hline \end{array}$

25. $7 \times 659 = $ ▨
26. $4 \times 375 = $ ▨
27. $5 \times 640 = $ ▨

28. $832 \times 8 = $ ▨
29. $486 \times 6 = $ ▨
30. $298 \times 3 = $ ▨

PROBLEM SOLVING

31. Timer Watch Company makes 739 watches each day. How many watches are made in 6 days?

★ 32. Mrs. Lorenzo's jewelry store sold 135 watches in 4 weeks. Mr. Gold's store sold 127 watches during those weeks. Which store sold more watches?

Mrs. Lorenzo kept this record of watches that her store bought. Copy and complete it.

	Number of Watches	Cost of Each Watch	Total Cost
	8	$52	$416
33.	2	$35	▨
34.	7	$120	▨
35.	3	$149	▨

Multiplying 4-digit Numbers

A. A shirt company made 2,840 shirts.
There were 4 buttons on each shirt.
How many buttons were used?

2,840 sets of 4.

Do:
$$
\begin{array}{r}
\overset{\text{③①}}{2{,}840} \\
\times4 \\
\hline
11{,}360
\end{array}
$$

11,360 buttons were used.

B. The Shirt Store sold 4 shirts
for $22.95 each. How much
did the store receive for the shirts?

1 shirt ↔ $22.95
4 shirts ↔ 4 sets of $22.95

$4 \times \$22.95 = $ ▩

$$
\begin{array}{r}
\overset{\text{①③②}}{\$22.95} \\
\times4 \\
\hline
\$91.80
\end{array}
$$

• • • $22.95 = 2295¢

The store received $91.80.

TRY THESE

Find each product.

1. 8,316
    × 4

2. 3,891
    × 6

3. 2,180
    × 5

4. 2,903
    × 8

5. 856
    × 6

SKILLS PRACTICE

Find each product.

1. 1,605
    × 4

2. 2,147
    × 6

3. 2,012
    × 8

4. 453
    × 3

5. 1,875
    × 9

6. 9,517
    × 7

7. 7,156
    × 5

8. 8,495
    × 2

9. 640
    × 8

10. 8,000
    × 4

11. 1,205
    × 5

12. 87
    × 9

13. 7,006
    × 6

14. 832
    × 3

15. 3,528
    × 7

16. 2,962
    × 4

17. 7,219
    × 6

18. 8,437
    × 2

19. 1,680
    × 5

20. 311
    × 7

21. 568
    × 3

22. 2,844
    × 9

23. 72
    × 8

24. 9,503
    × 5

25. 8,996
    × 7

26. $3 \times 2{,}879 =$ ▧

27. $6 \times 5{,}109 =$ ▧

28. $8 \times 5{,}417 =$ ▧

29. $4 \times 6{,}300 =$ ▧

30. $2 \times 759 =$ ▧

31. $9 \times 7{,}153 =$ ▧

32. $2{,}713 \times 5 =$ ▧

33. $8{,}505 \times 6 =$ ▧

34. $3{,}561 \times 8 =$ ▧

PROBLEM SOLVING

35. The Classic Shirt Company made 4,819 shirts. Each shirt has 2 pockets. How many pockets are there?

36. The shirt company sold 750 shirts to a store. The company charged $6 for each shirt. How much did the store pay for the shirts?

37. Casual Shirt Company made 4,318 shirts. Each shirt has 9 buttons. How many buttons were used?

★38. The company made 2,107 flannel and 2,211 cotton shirts. How many shirts did it make? It sold 789 flannel and 864 cotton shirts. How many shirts did it sell? How many shirts were left?

Changing Metric Units

Sometimes you need to change the unit used in the report of a measure. The facts shown in this table will help you.

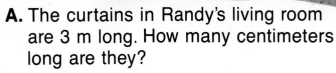

1 meter (m) = 100 centimeters (cm)
1 kilometer (km) = 1,000 meters (m)
1 liter (L) = 1,000 milliliters (mL)
1 kilogram (kg) = 1,000 grams (g)

A. The curtains in Randy's living room are 3 m long. How many centimeters long are they?

1 m = 100 cm

$$3 \text{ m} = 3 \times 1 \text{ m}$$
$$= 3 \times 100 \text{ cm}$$
$$= 300 \text{ cm}$$

The curtains are 300 cm long.

B. Randy's family drank 2 L of milk yesterday. How many milliliters of milk did they drink?

1 L = 1,000 mL

$$2 \text{L} = 2 \times 1 \text{ L}$$
$$= 2 \times 1,000 \text{ mL}$$
$$= 2,000 \text{ mL}$$

They drank 2,000 mL of milk yesterday.

TRY THESE

Find the missing numbers.

1. 9 kg = ▧ g

2. 5 m = ▧ cm

3. 8 km = ▧ m

SKILLS PRACTICE

Find the missing numbers.

1. 8 L = ▨ mL

2. 5 km = ▨ m

3. 9 m = ▨ cm

4. 2 kg = ▨ g

5. 4 L = ▨ mL

6. 6 km = ▨ m

7. 8 m = ▨ cm

8. 5 m = ▨ cm

9. 6 kg = ▨ g

10. 3 L = ▨ mL

11. 7 km = ▨ m

12. 3 m = ▨ cm

PROBLEM SOLVING

13. 3 kg is how many grams?

14. 7 L is how many milliliters?

15. 6 m is how many centimeters?

16. 4 kilometers is how many meters?

17. A turkey has a mass of 8 kg. What is its mass in grams?

18. The bag of groceries has a mass of 5 kg. What is its mass in grams?

19. Cliff rode his bicycle 9 km on Saturday. How many meters did he ride?

20. The rug in Margot's room is 2 m long. How many centimeters long is the rug?

★21. The Frazier family drank 2 L of milk on Saturday and 3 L of milk on Sunday. How many liters did they drink during the weekend? How many milliliters of milk did they drink during the weekend?

★22. The Martinez family drank 2 L of milk on Monday, 850 mL on Tuesday, and 1 L on Wednesday. How many milliliters of milk did the family drink in these 3 days?

EXTRA! Using a Pattern
Look at the following pattern.
Then find the missing numbers.

1,000 grams = 1 kilogram

6,000 grams = ▨ kilograms

2,000 grams = 2 kilograms

7,000 grams = ▨ kilograms

3,000 grams = 3 kilograms

8,000 grams = ▨ kilograms

4,000 grams = ▨ kilograms

9,000 grams = ▨ kilograms

5,000 grams = 5 kilograms

10,000 grams = ▨ kilograms

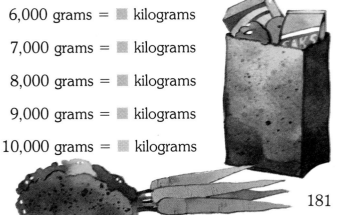

Problem Solving: Too Much Information

1 Read the problem.
2 Plan what to do.
3 Do the arithmetic.
4 Give the answer.
5 Check your answer.

You must choose only the information you need when too much information is given.

The toy store sold kites and balloons. Each balloon cost $.59. Each kite cost $1.29. Juan bought 4 kites. How much did he spend?

Must find: How much Juan spent.

Know: He bought 4 kites.
        1 kite costs $1.29.
        1 balloon costs $.59.

You *do not* need to use the cost of a balloon since Juan bought only kites.

$$1 \text{ kite} \leftrightarrow \$1.29 \qquad \$1.29$$
$$4 \text{ kites} \leftrightarrow 4 \times \$1.29 \qquad \underline{\times \quad 4}$$
$$\$5.16$$

Juan spent $5.16.

TRY THESE

Find the facts you need. Solve the problems.

1. Eric had $50.00. He bought 5 model airplanes. Each cost $7.00. How much did he spend all together?

2. Sue made $17.00 by babysitting for 8 hours. She wanted to buy a game that costs $23.98. How much more money does she need?

3. Joan bought 3 kites. Each kite was 24 inches long and cost $1.79. How much did she spend?

4. George had $20.00. He bought a game of checkers for $4.98 and a chess set for $13.00. How much did he spend?

PROBLEM SOLVING PRACTICE _____

Find the facts you need. Solve each problem.

1. Sam had $70.00. He bought 3 toy robots for $13.95 each. How much did he spend in all?

2. A 5-car train set costs $35.98. A 6-car racing set costs $27.49. How much more does the train set cost?

3. Virginia bought a toy computer with 26 keys for $7.98 and a battery for $.69. How much did she spend in all?

4. Eli bought 4 model 217-2 racing cars. Each car cost $5.47. How much did Eli spend for racing cars?

5. Mr. Willis has 5 children. Their ages are 3, 5, 6, 8, and 11. He bought each of them a kite for $1.49 each. How much did he spend in all?

6. On Monday, 13 shoppers spent $98.71 in the toy store. On Tuesday, 7 shoppers spent $91.16. How much money did they spend in all?

7. Mrs. Rosen bought 6 small beach balls. Large beach balls cost $2.00 each. Small beach balls cost $1.30 each. How much did she spend in all?

8. Lori went to the toy store with $20.00. She bought 2 puzzles and spent $3.59 in all. How much money did she have left?

★9. Alice bought 3 model cars for $6.98 each. How much did she spend for cars? She bought a 5-ounce tube of glue for $.89. How much did she spend in all?

★10. David bought a 30-inch by 30-inch easel for $25.00. He bought 8 tubes of paint for $1.49 each. How much did he spend in all?

EXTRA! Following Instructions
Gino built this magic box. When he put 5 into the box, it gave him the answer 132. What answer will it give if he puts 2 into the box? 4? 7?

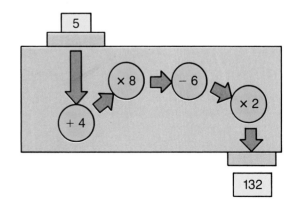

Unit Checkup

Multiply. *(pages 166–171)*

1. 23
   × 3

2. 38
   × 5

3. 51
   × 2

4. 86
   × 4

5. 30
   × 9

6. 42
   × 6

7. 63
   × 3

8. 49
   × 7

9. 33
   × 8

10. 70
    × 6

11. 18
    × 5

12. 29
    × 9

13. $71 \times 4 = $ ▩

14. $2 \times 97 = $ ▩

15. $36 \times 8 = $ ▩

16. $59 \times 5 = $ ▩

17. $3 \times 32 = $ ▩

18. $92 \times 8 = $ ▩

Multiply. *(pages 174–177)*

19. 413
    × 3

20. 127
    × 3

21. 240
    × 4

22. 319
    × 6

23. 485
    × 6

24. 509
    × 7

25. 681
    × 5

26. 789
    × 9

27. 452
    × 5

28. 611
    × 7

29. 827
    × 8

30. 566
    × 9

31. $6 \times 800 = $ ▩

32. $7 \times 952 = $ ▩

33. $3 \times 137 = $ ▩

34. $149 \times 5 = $ ▩

35. $548 \times 6 = $ ▩

36. $369 \times 8 = $ ▩

Multiply. *(pages 178–179)*

37. 4,312
    × 2

38. 6,013
    × 5

39. 1,390
    × 4

40. 5,619
    × 7

41. 2,032
    × 4

42. 3,987
    × 6

43. 7,941
    × 3

44. 5,214
    × 8

45. 1,808
    × 7

46. 3,276
    × 9

47. $4 \times 8,372 = $ ▩

48. $6 \times 9,500 = $ ▩

49. $3 \times 5,692 = $ ▩

50. $5 \times 4,905 = $ ▩

51. $8 \times 1,148 = $ ▩

52. $9 \times 9,893 = $ ▩

Find each product. *(pages 178–179)*

53. 3,113
×　5

54. 7,601
×　7

55. 2,849
×　6

56. 2,568
×　8

57. 4,280
×　2

58. 6,985
×　3

59. 4,509
×　9

60. 1,494
×　4

61. 3,305
×　7

62. 7,500
×　4

63. $5 \times 8,391 = $ ■

64. $3 \times 6,009 = $ ■

65. $8 \times 3,600 = $ ■

66. $4 \times 8,806 = $ ■

67. $6 \times 1,252 = $ ■

68. $9 \times 2,781 = $ ■

Solve the problems. *(pages 166–171, 174–183)*

69. There are 28 cars on the roller coaster. 6 people can sit in each car. How many people can ride the roller coaster?

70. 27 people can ride on the ferris wheel at one time. 3 people can sit on each seat. How many seats are there?

71. 5 cars entered the fun house. 12 people sat in each car. How many people entered the fun house?

72. Joe spent $2.40 for food and $4.50 for rides. How much money did he spend?

73. 3,568 people entered the park. They each paid a $2 entrance fee. How much money was collected at the entrance?

74. On Monday, Allan spent $9.30 to buy 3 straw hats. On Tuesday, he spent $9.80 for souvenirs. How much money did he spend in all?

75. Ellen went on 4 roller coaster rides at the amusement park. Ferris wheel rides cost $.40. Roller coaster rides cost $.50. How much did she spend?

76. 1,370 people were in the amusement park. 7 more people came in. How many people were in the park then?

77. Patty walked 2 kilometers in the amusement park. How many meters did she walk?

78. The peanut man sold 8 kilograms of peanuts. How many grams of peanuts did he sell?

185

More Help with Multiplication

Multiply.

324
× 2
648

1. 23
× 3

2. 10
× 8

3. 32
× 3

4. 38
× 1

5. 221
× 4

6. 132
× 3

7. 404
× 2

8. 314
× 2

①
1,007
× 2
2,014

9. 19
× 5

10. 25
× 3

11. 36
× 2

12. 124
× 3

13. 206
× 4

14. 119
× 4

15. 137
× 2

16. 2,114
× 5

②①
164
× 4
656

17. 56
× 3

18. 32
× 5

19. 84
× 4

20. 187
× 3

21. 296
× 2

22. 158
× 6

23. 136
× 6

24. 1,249
× 3

①②①
4,342
× 5
21,710

25. 538
× 4

26. 629
× 5

27. 227
× 8

28. 483
× 4

29. 935
× 3

30. 2,357
× 4

31. 1,382
× 5

32. 5,351
× 6

Tree Diagrams

A sandwich shop has white and rye bread. It has tuna salad, chicken salad, and egg salad. If the cook uses only one kind of bread and one kind of spread at a time, how many different kinds of sandwiches can be made?

Draw a *tree diagram* to find the number of different kinds of sandwiches.

Bread	Spread	Sandwich
white	→tuna salad ⟶	→ white bread, tuna salad
	→chicken salad ⟶	→ white bread, chicken salad
	→egg salad ⟶	→ white bread, egg salad
rye	→tuna salad ⟶	→ rye bread, tuna salad
	→chicken salad ⟶	→ rye bread, chicken salad
	→egg salad ⟶	→ rye bread, egg salad

The cook can make 6 different kinds of sandwiches with 2 kinds of bread and 3 kinds of spread.

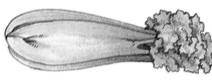

Draw a tree diagram to answer each question.

1. How many kinds of sandwiches can be made using white bread, or rye bread, or whole wheat bread with peanut butter, or cheese, or turkey?

2. How many different outfits can you make if you have 3 pairs of pants and 4 shirts?

3. How many different outfits can you make if you have 2 shirts, 2 pairs of jeans, and 2 belts?

4. Can you think of a way to answer Exercises 1–3 without drawing tree diagrams?

Maintaining Skills

Choose the correct answer.

1.

a. $.45
b. $4.50
c. $.35
d. not given

2.

a. $3.10
b. $.21
c. $.25
d. not given

3. 6)‾40

a. 6 R3
b. 5
c. 6 R4
d. not given

4. 8)‾47

a. 5 R3
b. 5 R7
c. 5 R4
d. not given

5. 6)‾42

a. 6
b. 7 R2
c. 7 R4
d. not given

6. 8)‾67

a. 8 R2
b. 8 R3
c. 8
d. not given

7. 7)‾59

a. 8 R3
b. 8 R2
c. 8
d. not given

8. 9)‾87

a. 9
b. 9 R5
c. 9 R6
d. not given

9.
$$\begin{array}{r} 976 \\ \times\ \ 8 \\ \hline \end{array}$$

a. 7,088
b. 7,808
c. 7,768
d. not given

10.
$$\begin{array}{r} 796 \\ \times\ \ 6 \\ \hline \end{array}$$

a. 4,776
b. 4,767
c. 4,746
d. not given

11.
$$\begin{array}{r} 948 \\ \times\ \ 7 \\ \hline \end{array}$$

a. 6,663
b. 6,686
c. 6,336
d. not given

12.
$$\begin{array}{r} 8,675 \\ \times\ \ \ \ \ 9 \\ \hline \end{array}$$

a. 78,705
b. 78,075
c. 78,035
d. not given

13. A truck delivered 81 boxes to 9 stores. Each store received the same number of boxes. How many boxes did each store receive?

a. 10 boxes   b. 9 boxes
c. 8 boxes   d. not given

14. Mr. King owns a bakery. Each day Mr. King bakes 144 rolls. How many rolls can he bake in 7 days?

a. 1,108 rolls   b. 1,008 rolls
c. 988 rolls   d. not given

MID-YEAR REVIEW: Skills

Add.

1. 4
  +3

2. 0
  +0

3. 1
  +7

4. 0
  +6

5. 3
  +5

6. 7
  +3

7. 6
  +1

8. 2
  +7

9. 5
  +9

10. 8
  +5

11. 4
  +5

12. 8
  +9

13. 4
  +9

14. 5
  +5

15. $2 + 9 = \blacksquare$

16. $6 + 3 = \blacksquare$

17. $7 + 5 = \blacksquare$

Subtract.

18. 1
  −0

19. 9
  −6

20. 7
  −7

21. 5
  −3

22. 6
  −0

23. 9
  −4

24. 7
  −2

25. 13
  − 4

26. 8
  −1

27. 10
  − 7

28. 11
  − 4

29. 17
  − 8

30. 14
  − 7

31. 16
  − 7

32. $9 − 1 = \blacksquare$

33. $13 − 6 = \blacksquare$

34. $15 − 9 = \blacksquare$

Show how to read each standard numeral.

35. 73,216

36. 493,060

37. 219,000

Write the numerals.

38. five thousand three hundred forty-seven
39. four hundred twenty-nine thousand six hundred eighty-three
40. eighteen thousand
41. one hundred nine thousand six

Round a. to the nearest ten; b. to the nearest hundred.

a.	638 $\longrightarrow$ 640
b.	638 $\longrightarrow$ 600

42. 603

43. 251

44. 894

45. 96

Add.

476
+839 ⟨1 1⟩
_____
1,315

46. 36
+42

47. 57
+68

48. 507
+392

49. 938
+215

50. 436
+491

51. $5.73
+ 5.68

52. $37.48
+ 42.61

53. 3,276
+8,673

54. 17,134 + 2,695 = ▓

55. 568 + 20,649 = ▓

56. 8,436 + 93,596 = ▓

57. 86 + 249 + 517 = ▓

58. 2,739 + 856 + 718 + 5,069 = ▓

Subtract.

$7.01 ⟨9 6 10 11⟩
− 4.95
_____
$ 2.06

59. 86
−25

60. 73
− 9

61. 260
− 74

62. 642
−533

63. 103
− 85

64. $5.00
− 1.08

65. $12.35
− 1.32

66. 6,403
−6,371

67. $30.50 − $15.35 = ▓

68. 7,340 − 6,585 = ▓

69. $12.00 − $9.72 = ▓

70. 9,004 − 1,327 = ▓

71. 17,046 − 8,432 = ▓

72. 40,000 − 10,703 = ▓

Multiply.

73. 1
×1

74. 7
×2

75. 0
×0

76. 5
×4

77. 2
×2

78. 1
×5

79. 3
×3

80. 9
×3

81. 4
×2

82. 8
×5

83. 3
×7

84. 5
×0

85. 7
×4

86. 3
×1

87. 2
×6

88. 8
×8

89. 0
×4

90. 2
×8

91. 6
×9

92. 4
×6

93. 5
×7

Complete the number sentences.

94. $0 \times 8 =$ ▓

95. $5 \times 6 =$ ▓

96. $9 \times 9 =$ ▓

97. ▓ $\times 7 = 42$

98. ▓ $\times 9 = 63$

99. ▓ $\times 6 = 48$

Divide.

$$8\overline{)35} \quad \begin{array}{r} 4 \text{ R3} \\ \hline 35 \\ 32 \\ \hline 3 \end{array}$$

100. $4\overline{)16}$ **101.** $3\overline{)15}$ **102.** $6\overline{)18}$ **103.** $5\overline{)10}$

104. $3\overline{)10}$ **105.** $7\overline{)21}$ **106.** $9\overline{)30}$ **107.** $8\overline{)70}$

108. $7\overline{)56}$ **109.** $6\overline{)32}$ **110.** $3\overline{)26}$ **111.** $5\overline{)43}$

112. $28 \div 4 = \blacksquare$ **113.** $18 \div 2 = \blacksquare$ **114.** $54 \div 9 = \blacksquare$

Find the total value.

							Total Value
115.			2	1	2	3	$\blacksquare$
116.		1	1	2	1		$\blacksquare$
117.	1	3	2	1	3	2	$\blacksquare$
118.		4		1	2	4	$\blacksquare$
119.	1		6	3	4	7	$\blacksquare$

Read each clock.

120.

$\blacksquare:\blacksquare$

$\blacksquare$ minutes to $\blacksquare$

121.

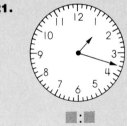

$\blacksquare:\blacksquare$

$\blacksquare$ minutes past $\blacksquare$

122.

$\blacksquare:\blacksquare$

$\blacksquare$ minutes to $\blacksquare$

Multiply.

$$\begin{array}{r} ⑦④ \\ 796 \\ \times \quad 8 \\ \hline 6{,}368 \end{array}$$

123. $\begin{array}{r} 23 \\ \times\ 3 \\ \hline \end{array}$ **124.** $\begin{array}{r} 60 \\ \times\ 4 \\ \hline \end{array}$ **125.** $\begin{array}{r} 94 \\ \times\ 5 \\ \hline \end{array}$ **126.** $\begin{array}{r} 58 \\ \times\ 8 \\ \hline \end{array}$ **127.** $\begin{array}{r} 9 \\ \times73 \\ \hline \end{array}$

128. $\begin{array}{r} 147 \\ \times\ 6 \\ \hline \end{array}$ **129.** $\begin{array}{r} 850 \\ \times\ 6 \\ \hline \end{array}$ **130.** $\begin{array}{r} 609 \\ \times\ 9 \\ \hline \end{array}$ **131.** $\begin{array}{r} 4 \\ \times238 \\ \hline \end{array}$ **132.** $\begin{array}{r} 324 \\ \times\ 7 \\ \hline \end{array}$

133. $3 \times 3{,}142 = \blacksquare$ **134.** $8 \times 2{,}900 = \blacksquare$ **135.** $3{,}572 \times 7 = \blacksquare$

191

MID-YEAR REVIEW: Problem Solving

A. Kai used 336 cm of string to wrap one package and 418 cm of string to wrap a second package. How much string did he use in all?

Add to find how much in all.

```
      1
    336
  +418
    754
```

He used 754 cm of string in all.

B. Kai spent $2.59 to mail the first package and $5.00 to mail the second. How much less did he spend for the first than for the second?

Subtract to find how much less.

```
        9
    4 10 10
  $ 5.0 0
  - 2.5 9
  $ 2.4 1
```

He spent $2.41 less for the first.

C. 3,741 packages were mailed at the post office. 2,914 were sent first class. The others were sent book rate. How many were sent book rate?

Subtract to find how many were sent book rate.

```
  2 17 3 11
   3,7 4 1
  -2,9 1 4
     8 2 7
```

827 packages were sent book rate.

D. The mass of each carton a store shipped was 36 kg. What was the total mass of their shipment, if they shipped 9 cartons?

Multiply to find the total mass.

```
     ⑤
    36
   × 9
   324
```

1 carton ⟷ 36 kg

9 cartons ⟷ 9 sets of 36 kg

The total mass was 324 kg.

E. The total shipping cost of 9 packages was $72. It cost the same amount to ship each package. What was the cost of shipping each package?

Divide to find the cost for each.

```
      8
  9)72
    72
     0
```

9 packages ⟷ $72

1 package ⟷ ■

It cost $8 to ship each package.

1. There were 18 boats on the lake. Then 7 more boats sailed onto the lake. How many boats were on the lake?

2. There were 103 ducks on the lake. Then 87 ducks flew away. How many ducks were still on the lake?

3. Mr. Jackson received 5 boxes of books. There were 8 books in each box. How many books did he receive?

4. Mrs. Stevens had $120 and went shopping. When she got home, she had $35 left. How much did she spend?

5. Mary started with $12.50. Then she collected $27.85 from the customers on her paper route. How much money did she have then?

6. Joe wants to buy a book of maps that costs $15. He has $6. How much more money does he need?

7. Sally has 29 cards. She puts 4 in each envelope. How many envelopes can she use? How many cards will be left over?

8. A store had a red ribbon 40 m long. A piece 12 m long was cut off and sold. How long was the ribbon that was left?

9. John read 9 pages of a science fiction story before dinner and 8 pages after dinner. How many pages did he read?

10. A coat in Store A costs $52. The same kind of coat costs $45 in Store B. How much more is the cost of the coat in Store A than in Store B?

11. During the month of May, Mr. Hanson made 7 trips. Each trip was a distance of 750 km. How far did he travel all together?

12. The Weavers bought a sofa for $253 and a chair for $142. How much did they spend for this furniture?

13. Mr. Kells has $35 and buys shirts which cost $7 each. What is the largest number of shirts he can buy?

14. At the March town meeting the attendance was 1,438 people, at the April town meeting the attendance was 1,783, and at the May town meeting the attendance was 1,693. What was the total attendance for these meetings?

15. The distance from Joan's home to school was 850 m. Pedro lived 620 m from school. How many more meters from school did Joan live than did Pedro?

16. In an election, 5,200 votes were cast. Ms. Trent received 2,750 of the votes. How many votes were not for Ms. Trent?

17. A scout troop hiked 12 km before lunch and 16 km after lunch. How far did the troop hike?

18. A small bus carries 18 passengers when full. How many passengers can be carried on 8 trips?

19. Lon has 24 roses and 3 vases. He puts the same number of roses in each vase. How many roses can he put into each vase? How many roses will be left over?

20. There are 370 students in Warren School and 495 students in Polk School. How many fewer students are there in Warren School than in Polk School?

21. It took 3 buses to carry 125 people to the circus. Each bus ticket cost $6. How much did it cost for all 125 tickets?

22. Ms. Johnson spent $36 for 4 sweaters. Each sweater was the same price. How much did each sweater cost?

23. Bill keeps a record of the money he has. He adds the money he earns and subtracts the money he spends. Complete Bill's record.

24. A store sells different kinds of shirts at different prices. Complete the table.

Date	Earned	Spent	Has
July 5	$5.60		$5.60
July 6		$3.17	▨
July 7	$2.75		▨
July 8		$1.53	▨
July 9		$2.08	▨
July 10	$3.90		▨

Number of shirts	Cost of each shirt	Total cost
2	$12	$24
3	$ 8	▨
6	$13	▨
5	$15	▨